Love Notes in Lunchboxes

And Other Ideas
to Color Your Child's Day

Linda J. Gilden

n e w
hope
PUBLISHERS

Birmingham, Alabama

New Hope® Publishers
P. O. Box 12065
Birmingham, AL 35202-2065
www.newhopepublishers.com

Library of Congress Cataloging-in-Publication Data

ISBN: 1-56309-821-0

N044109 • 0904 • 8.5M1

Dedication

To my husband John, my partner in life and lunchbox preparation. Not only are you my head cheerleader but you have been cook, chauffeur, grocery shopper, reader, and much more during the writing of this book. For that and so many other reasons, I love you and thank God for you. Only He could have created such a wonderful helpmate for me.

To Kristi, Jim, Ginger, and Jeff, note recipients who bless my life. I treasure each one of you, my precious children. Thank you for your love, support, ideas, willingness to be the "stars" of my writing, and for the love notes you have left me along the way.

There are not enough love notes in the world to express my love for each of you!

Table of Contents

Acknowledgments. 6
Introduction 7

Chapter One:
Love Notes Make a Difference. 9
> Love notes written to your children can be the building
> blocks for self-esteem, self-confidence, and character.

Chapter Two:
Special Days. 41
> Try some of these creative ideas for making lunch
> festive on holidays, birthdays, game days, and
> every day.

Chapter Three:
Christmas in the Lunchbox. 75
> Along with decking the halls and walls of your home,
> enjoy creative ideas for decorating your child's lunchbox.

Chapter Four:
Love Notes Touch Others. 89
> Love notes included in your child's lunch may
> also be a bright spot in someone else's day.

Chapter Five:
Love Notes Provide a Little Extra Love.........97

When your child needs a little extra encouragement,
your love notes can be a lifeline.

Chapter Six:
Other Types of Love Notes...............113

Notes don't always have to be words on paper!
Creative ways to say "I love you" abound in this
section of innovative love notes for all ages.

Chapter Seven:
Beyond the Lunchbox 149

College kids and adult children also need to know
they are loved. Try a few of these ideas for making
children who have left the lunchbox behind feel
special.

Appendix 167

Tips on how to write special love notes,
instructions for creating fun lunchbox fare, and blank
notes you can copy and personalize.

Acknowledgments

To Becky Yates and Rebecca England and all the wonderful New Hope staff—thank you for believing in me and for your commitment to sharing God's message with excellence.

To Dalene Parker, Angie Rosenlund, Candy Arrington, Sylvia Caldwell, Jimmie Davis, Sheila Sistare, Joyce Morgan, Met Schrieffer, Michele Brady, Papoo, John, Kristi, Ginger, and Jeff—thank you for taking the time to read, pray, and help make *Love Notes in Lunchboxes* the very best it can be.

To all the "lunchbox kids" who so freely shared how lunchbox love notes have touched their lives—thank you.

Introduction

The story of Jesus feeding the five thousand on the shore of the Sea of Galilee is told in all four Gospels. The crowd had listened to Jesus teach for many hours and had become hungry. The disciples began to question one another, "Where shall we buy bread for these people to eat?" (John 6:5) All four Gospels report that the only rations to be found were five small loaves of barley and two fish. Jesus used these loaves and fish to perform one of the His best-known miracles. But where did they come from?

Only John tells us. Those five loaves and two fish came from a little boy's lunchbox. His mother knew he would be hungry. Although she didn't realize it, she was providing the things Jesus would need to perform one of the best-known miracles of His ministry.

Don't you wish you could do something so important? You can.

If you have children, you could be their primary source of encouragement and healthy self-esteem. Maybe you feel your time is limited because of work responsibilities. Maybe you are a single parent. No matter what your daily schedule, you can snatch a few seconds each day to encourage those most precious to you. And you can do it in a lunchbox.

For many years, my children carried a lunchbox or bag to school. At our house, it was a team effort—Dad fixed the lunch while I wrote the note. Each day they had a carefully prepared sandwich, fruit, maybe some chips, and a cookie. But the most important thing in the lunchbox was not the food. It was the note!

Chapter One

Love Notes
Make a Difference

The idea of taking food along when you are going to be away from home during mealtime is not new. A little boy's lunch during biblical times provided the elements necessary for one of Jesus' best-known miracles. Workers have long carried nourishment to their workplaces.

In the early 1950s, consumer product advertisers began targeting children with their products. One of the most popular was the lunchbox. The practicality of the box combined with television characters and heroes on the outside of the lunchbox contributed to its success and popularity.

Lunchboxes have come a long way since their first rise to popularity. The '50s introduced metal boxes, which were followed by plastic ones. Because of a mothers' campaign in Florida, metal lunchboxes ceased to be manufactured after the early seventies because of the danger! This group of mothers felt the metal lunchbox could be used as a weapon and may cause injury to a child.

Lunchboxes are now available in many colors, shapes, and sizes and have varied designs on the outside depicting characters and interests. The late summer shopping trip to pick out a new lunchbox was always a special occasion at our house.

But what should be included on the inside? Here are a few suggestions.

THE ENTRÉE—A sandwich, pasta, leftover chicken, some dry cereal . . . the list is endless. Just make sure it is something that your children like and is not too messy to eat! Periodically surprise them with something out of the ordinary.

A "SIDE ITEM"—Cut-up veggies, chips, or a combination will work.

FRUIT—This will provide extra vitamins as well as carbohydrates that will be used for energy.

DESSERT—If your child enjoys something sweet at the end of the meal, include a granola bar, cookie, cereal bar, or a homemade treat. Or omit this item and let the fruit be the finishing touch to lunch!

DRINK—Some lunchboxes come with a thermos; others do not. Water, fruit juices, and other drinks now come in disposable bottles or boxes that are easily packed in the lunchbox.

If your child has special needs, the menu must be adjusted to those, of course. This is much more easily done in a lunchbox than when your child eats a cafeteria lunch. When you have assembled all the physical food to put in the lunchbox, there is only one more thing to put in . . . the note!

THE NOTE—This is the most important thing in the lunchbox. A short "love note" may be the only morsel of encouragement received during those school hours. And those morsels are being stored and will bind together in the heart of your child to develop character and self-esteem. Hopefully, lunchbox notes will also be laying the groundwork for a lifetime of faith in God.

A Lunchbox Kid Says

When I was going into kindergarten, my mom decided to get me a new lunch box. It was pink and had purple and yellow flowers all over it. After taking it over to my dad so he could write my name on it, I found out that the lunch box had a thermos to match. I thought I was the coolest thing around because I could take whatever kind of drink to school and the teacher wouldn't know . . . but that wasn't the thing that caught my eye. When you turned the lunchbox over, it had a "message window" on it. My mom would always leave me notes in it and it just made me happy to know that I got a note from her, even if all it had on it was a smiley face . . . just to know that your parents love you is one of the greatest feelings in the world.

—Jennifer, age 20

Parental Affirmation

"Parental affirmation is a gift all children need. One of the most positive things parents can do to impact their children is to speak blessings," says Dr. David W. Cox, Christian family counselor. "Children who receive encouragement and blessing from their parents do not seek validation in potentially destructive ways as teens."

Children are never too young or too old to be told they are loved. And there are many ways to communicate your love to them. There are the obvious ways of showing your affection by hugging, kissing, patting them on the back, and just saying the words "I love you." But if you put it in a note, you are not just giving them affirmation for a moment; they can save your notes and reread them when they need a little lift.

Notes do not have to be long, but no matter what the words the message is still the same: "You are special. I'm glad we have each other."

First grade notes can be very simple. Use pictures, single letters, or a combination. Even a nonreader will get the message!

Middle schoolers need a little less obvious message. Slip a copy of a photograph of a special moment into the lunchbox. Attach a sticky note with a smiley face on it.

High schoolers are back to thinking it is cool just to get a note. Knock-knock jokes and trivia questions are especially welcome at this age because they like to pass the notes around the table.

Lunchbox Note
Draw an eye, a heart, and an upper case U.

It's Not the Words That Matter

"You know, Mom," Ginger said, "I don't really remember what you said in all those notes you wrote in my lunches. But I remember you wrote them and they always showed you cared. Some days I think all you said was, 'Have a good day' or 'You are special,' but it meant a lot. Just to know that you took the time to write a note and that you thought it was an important part of my lunch made my day. Most kids only had food in their lunch bags!"

Yes, the food is an essential part of the lunchbox. But even more important than the food for their bodies is the food for their spirits.

Physical growth does not occur in one spurt. It is the result of years of feeding and nurturing along with exercise and proper health maintenance. There is constant development and every small bit of nutrition contributes to growth.

Spiritual growth is the same way. But before we can help our children to grow, we must introduce them to the Savior. Before they can even begin to develop a spiritual life, they must have an experience with God. As parents, we can show them God's way by example and through words. Then when they are old enough to understand the process of salvation, they will be ready to accept it as their own.

Notes in the lunchbox can be some of the building blocks that bring your child to know Jesus. Then your notes can be stepping-stones on a journey toward knowing Jesus better and understanding who God has created your child to be.

A few lunchbox words can do that? Yes, absolutely! In the early years, lunchbox notes cannot be wordy because of your child's reading level. But even a daily "I love you" teaches your child about the love of a parent and ultimately about the love of his Heavenly Father.

When your child begins to read, your continued affirmation does this with words like "You are special!" and "There is no one like you. You're the best!" As your child gets older, short verses of Scripture or prayers can be added.

Lunchbox notes may not be the method by which God brings your child to Him, but notes can lay the foundation that will bring forth that experience in your child's life. They will keep the lines of spiritual dialogue flowing and invite your child to come to you with questions about God.

Lunchbox notes can build character, self-confidence, and self-esteem. They can encourage your child to put God first. Just a few words that may not even be remembered can have a tremendous impact on your child's life.

A Lunchbox Kid Says

My dad said, "See you tonight. We'll have a great time. Love, Dad." I wanted to hurry home!

—Caleb, age 9

It's Biblical

Moses knew the importance of impressing God's laws on children. Deuteronomy 6:5–7, 9 says, "Love the Lord your God with all your heart and with all your soul and with all your strength. These commandments that I give you today are to be upon your hearts. Impress them on your children. Talk about them when you sit at home and when you walk along the road, when you lie down and when you get up. . . . Write them on the doorframes of your houses and on your gates."

I have no doubt that if he had lived today, along with the doorframes and gates of the houses, Moses would have included the lunchbox as an appropriate place to write special nuggets of truth.

Spoken words are precious. But once heard, they are usually forgotten or, at best, only partially remembered. But a note can be treasured, reread, and tucked away in a special place. Days or even years later a note can be read again and rekindle the same original feelings—a smile at the feeling of being loved, a sense of determination upon a word of encouragement, a laugh at a word of enlightenment.

The more we encourage our children and implant God's love notes in their hearts, the more their love for Him will grow. And the closer our relationship with them will be.

A Lunchbox Kid Says

One day I was having a really bad day. When I got to lunch, I had a note from my mom. It really brightened my day. I felt better and could concentrate on my schoolwork. She also sends me cards to let me know she is praying for me.

—Brooke, age 13

Praise

In our home we have a cross-stitched sampler with just a few simple words—"Praise is a child's best vitamin." I don't know who the author of that phrase is, but it speaks volumes to me as a parent.

Praise does, indeed, often go further than a small dose of vitamins!

I remember one especially difficult parenting year. It seemed like my children were at the ages when everything they did needed some sort of adjustment! I felt like I was constantly fussing and we were not having any fun together.

After discussing it with my husband, we decided that for a week we would try to overlook the things that weren't perfect and find all the good things our children were doing. Some days that was very hard. Other days opportunities for praise abounded. It became a challenge for us and we wanted to succeed!

Some days we might say, "I'm so glad you remembered to put your bow in your hair. It matches your outfit nicely." What we really wanted to say was, "I think you need to go try combing your hair again. It looks like you missed a few spots. And while you are at it, straighten up the bow before it covers your entire ear!"

At the table, manners are always an issue. But instead of continuously saying, "Don't talk with your mouth full," and "Wipe your mouth before you get it all over your clothes," try finding a positive angle: "You really did a good job passing the potatoes," or "Thank you for taking your plate to the sink."

Praise helps children realize they are valued as people. It levels the ground a bit and encourages them to try harder to do the right thing. Most children really do want to please the adults in their lives. Many adults just forget to let them know when they do!

Lunchbox Note

You are full of surprises. Thank you for being such a great helper last night. Have a great day!

 A Lunchbox Kid Says

My mom has written me many messages in my suitcases and lunchboxes. One year on choir tour, she left probably 10 notes in my suitcase. It just made me know that she was still thinking about me and that she cared about me. It really made me thankful for

her. And I knew that she was praying for me, and if I got down, I knew she would be there when I got home.
—Wyatt, age 15

You're Special!

We all like to hear those words, "You are really special to me!" I don't think we can ever be told that enough. Every note conveys to your child that he or she is cherished. "The value of the spoken/written word makes you feel special," says Seth Buckley, minister to youth. "My boys will know that I love them and I cherish them because I have told them. And one way it is documented is through lunchbox love notes."

Making your child feel special doesn't have to be fancy or take a lot of time. It can be very simple and just say, "I love you. Have a good day," or "Can't wait to see you at 3 o'clock." Always include the note in the lunch . . . it's cheap, it's simple, low in fat and calories, and it will make your child's day!

Lunchbox Note

Look around you in the lunchroom. Do you know that you are the most special person in the whole room? I am so glad to be the mother of a special person!

A Lunchbox Kid Says

I admit to previewing my notes on the way to school just to boost my spirits. Sometimes my mother would write them the night before and insert into my lunch bag/box. I also admit to being so excited

17

about reading them that I would sometimes sneak
into my lunch the night before.

—Jaci, age 26

Staying Balanced

I watched Jeff as he ambled toward his classroom. I don't
guess second graders are ever in a hurry to get to school!
He walked down the driveway and just before he got to
the bottom of the hill, he spotted the curb.

Taking a few steps to the right, he mounted the "balance
beam," a challenge to be sure. I glanced at the clock. True, he
did have about ninety seconds before the late bell rang. But
was there really time for such antics on the way in? He continued slow acrobatic progress toward the portable classroom.

I watched as the weight of the backpack caused him to
teeter one way and then the other. His lunchbox was clutched
in one hand and his hat perched precariously on his head.
Despite my concern about the time, I savored those few extra
moments to watch my son. His enjoyment of the last few
moments of morning freedom made me smile! What a treasure!

Just before he hopped off of the "beam" and sprinted
toward the steps, he turned and smiled at me, obviously
pleased that I had been an audience of one.

I couldn't help think of my constant audience of One.
No matter what kind of antics or balancing acts I choose to
perform, there is One who is watching me, and He's probably
savoring the moment as He watches His child, too!

Lunchbox Note
*Keep your day balanced—study hard, listen in class, have
fun with your friends, and hurry home, 'cause I love you!*

Encouraging Your Child

"Mom, I don't even remember what most of my notes said." My twenty-something daughter was looking over my shoulder as I wrote. "But you know the neat thing? Even though I don't remember the exact words, I remember the feeling of opening that note and knowing how much you loved me! Other kids always waited to see what kind of note I had in my lunchbox. I didn't even have to read it because I knew what it meant. I might not have known the way you said it that day, but I knew that note said I was special. You always made me feel that way!"

Some days I was very original and spent time creating notes and puzzles and shopping for treats. Other days I just had to scribble a few words on the napkin. Whatever method I used for the day, evidently the message was loud and clear!

We all need to hear we are important to someone. We need to have our own personal cheerleaders, no matter how old we are or what we are trying to accomplish.

Recently I stopped at a traffic light. On the other side of the street was a large red SUV. All I could see was the driver. Suddenly, she began to nod her head and applaud wildly.

Upon a closer look, I could see the top of a car seat in the middle of the back seat. As the applause began, I could see movement from that direction.

What could have possibly happened to elicit so much applause? Maybe the toddler said "light" for the first time. Maybe the baby put his own pacifier back in his mouth without help. Maybe he was able to sing an entire verse of a song along with a CD that was playing.

All of these are certainly reasons for applause.

As our children get older, the things they learn get more difficult. They don't want us to applaud quite so loudly. But no matter what the age of your child, encouragement is needed. It may be in the form of applause or it may be in the form of a smile or a pat on the back. Whatever the form, give it out generously.

Kids can never get too much encouragement from the people who love them.

Lunchbox Note:
Hurray for you! You did a great job on your book report.
Isn't reading fun? Let's read a book together when you get home!
ILY (I love you)

A Lunchbox Kid Says

One way my mom showed me how much she loved me was through daily notes in my lunchbox—even through 12th grade!! It was a relief to have encouragement from home on a bad day, and it was very special to have that reminder of her love on a good day. She filled the notes with Scripture, and there was always a reminder that she was praying for me.

—Deb, age 19

Establishing Worth

If you enter any home that houses a preschooler, chances are the refrigerator will be full of hand drawn and colored pictures. There was a time in our family life when our refrigerator got so full we had to resort to taping artwork on the doors of the cabinets. Despite the fact that the art did not always match our décor, it was proudly displayed. Even paint-by-number pictures were allowed.

After the pictures have hung for a while, you tend to walk by them as if they are not there. Try to comment on your children's artistic efforts every now and then. It will be another building block in their life's foundation, even if they don't turn out to be professional artists!

A Lunchbox Kid Says

While I was fixing your lunch I noticed your artwork on the fridge. You really have an eye for color. Thanks for sharing it with us!

Love Notes for Fun—Katya Arrives

Ginger has always been a dramatic child. One year she took advanced drama, which meant that many of her activities in school and after school were related to drama. That was the year Katya came to live at our house!

Ginger was practicing her German accent one afternoon. No matter what we asked her, she replied in her new German accent. I walked up to her room to ask her a specific question.

"Ginger," I called, "I need to ask you something."

"I am not Ginger," she replied. "I am Katya."

"Katya?"

"Yah, my name eez Katya and I come from ze old country."

I stuck out my hand to shake hers. "Welcome to America. I hope you will be very happy here!"

That was my introduction to Katya. I thought Katya would be a quickly passing phase and if I just welcomed Katya to our family for a visit, she would eventually return to "ze old country." But Katya moved in and stayed for the rest of Ginger's school years. I will admit it was difficult to learn enough German words to write Katya notes. But she always appreciated the effort!

Lunchbox Note to Katya
You are ze most bootiful German girl I know.
I luff you so velly much. Haf a gut day.

More Fun—Katya's New Friend

It didn't take long for Katya to realize that she was lonely and needed a friend. That's when Rose became a special part of our family. One day Ginger was cleaning her room and I stopped at the door. In my best German accent I said, "Sank you, sank you. Eet ees so nize to haf you clean your room."

She looked up and said, "Oh, Rose, I am so glad to haf someone from my country. Where haf you been?"

"I haf been traveling ze world. I sought I vuld stop 'ere for a vee visit."

"Ah, come in, come in, and ve shall chat. Tell me ze news of ze old country."

This began a delightful afternoon of mother-daughter banter, banter that often resumes when I least expect it. I began to look for anything I could stick in Ginger's lunch that even hinted of "ze old country"—a piece of German chocolate cake, sauerkraut, a specific candy bar, anything that said, "I picked this especially for you."

Still today, Rose is a fixture in our family. She doesn't appear every day, but often. Rose's signature ending to her notes was her "logo," which she quickly developed. It was simply a squiggly line with a circle at the top and a few lines on the sides to resemble leaves—very crude, but always recognizable.

Rose's Lunchbox Note

Katya, I am so glad I stopped to see you. You haf a vunderful family, especially yo Muzzer. She eez so luffley and a great hostezz. I vill tell all ze folks in ze old country what a luffley family you haf. Haf a great day!

Building Relationships

Writing lunchbox notes to our children, expressing our love for them, creates pleasure, both for the writer and the recipient.

Notes give us an opportunity to write something that might be difficult to say in person, such as an affirmation or even an apology. Once those comments are made, the door is opened for further conversation.

How can notes help build relationships?

• To let your child know that you are on his side. Some days your child may arrive at lunch feeling he is a lone boat floating in a very large sea. Once he opens your note, however simple it may be, he knows that you are on his side.

• To open the door to a different type of communication. Many of us think we cannot write notes because we are not writers. That is simply not true! Most lunchbox notes include words learned during the first few years of school. And though their arrangement may not be eloquent, the heartfelt message is loud and clear.

• To allow opportunity to discuss things that are difficult. Your child may be having a difficult time with one of his

23

friends at school. Every time you bring up the subject, he clams up. But you want him to know that you care. Saying it in a note gives him the message but doesn't require discussion. Then, when your child is ready to talk about it, you will both have an open door.

• To let your child know that she is loved. Just including a note in the lunchbox says, "I care about you!"

Lunchbox Fact

If you pack a lunch for your child every day, first through twelfth grades, you will have packed around 2,160 lunches by graduation.

A Lunchbox Kid Says

Whenever I am really down and having a bad day, a note from my mom cheers me up. If I am in a really bad mood when I leave the house in the morning, when I get the note out of my lunchbox, it always makes my day. My mom's notes also help the friendship between me and my mom grow deeper.

—Shelley, age 13

Staying Connected

Each day has moments when we feel that we are standing alone. It doesn't matter if you are at the job where you have spent each day for the last forty years, or at school surrounded by a room full of friends, or at home in familiar territory—these feelings can occur. Often they are fleeting. But feeling like we are standing all alone against the world is difficult.

Just a short note in your child's lunchbox can help him feel that you are still connected even though you are, for the moment, at different locations. It will say to him, "You've still got someone on your side."

"I want family to be a part of what goes on at school," says Seth Buckley, father of four boys. "That can happen in the middle of the day when my boys read a love note. We can parent even when they are not around. The embrace of our love goes outside the home."

Continued communication throughout the day when you are physically separated will make the reconnection easier and quicker when you get back together.

Love notes will also allow you to continue a conversation started at an earlier time. You may feel the need to say one more thing, not to have the last word, but to reinforce praise of your child. An extra "I am proud of you" can go a long way.

Lunchbox Note
I really enjoy your company. Let's spend
some time together when we get home.

A Lunchbox kid Says

From the fifth to the seventh grade I carried a lunchbox. Every day my mom used to send me a note telling me she loved me and reminding me of what I had to do. She always comforted me and made me wonder what I would do without her fixing my lunch and writing me notes to strengthen my day.

—Jenni Lynn, age 15

Truthfulness

When two of our daughters were in junior high school, they rode to school with their dad. One morning Dad turned into the school to let them out. He had the right of way but another parent, Sue, seemed to think she should have been allowed to turn in first. After arriving on school grounds, Dad pulled over to the curb to let the children out of the car. Sue rammed her car into the side of Dad's car.

Several weeks later, we took the children to court with us, thinking this would be a great learning experience. We sat on the back row as men in shackles and handcuffs paraded in front of us for their cases to be heard. Each time one walked back, the children were wide-eyed.

"Hey, Mom, what did he do?"

"I'm not sure exactly what it was. He probably stole from someone, didn't respect someone else's property, or maybe got in a fight."

Whatever those men and women did, they were visual examples of the consequences of bad character for my very impressionable children. When time came for our case to be heard, Sue took the stand first. Under oath and after only one question, she began a false account of the incident.

"Mom, that's not what happened. Let me go up there and tell them what really happened," Kristi said.

"You can't let her get away with that, Dad," added Ginger.

"Shh!" whispered Dad. "We must respect that it is Sue's turn to speak. We will have a chance to tell our story."

As the officer in charge questioned both parents, it became obvious only one could be telling the truth. Everyone in the courtroom knew they were witnessing character on display, both good and bad.

Sue had no qualms about twisting the facts as she spoke. Evidently, lying under oath was permissible for her. After all, she was looking out for *her* best interests. She did not want to be charged in the case. If she lost this case, she would be responsible for car repairs and her insurance would go up. Not to mention she would have a documented case of road rage on her record.

Somewhere in Sue's past there was a gap. Someone had not successfully taught her the lessons of honesty, trustworthiness, caring, and respect. On the other hand, Dad respected Sue as a person and her right to state her case. Dad sat silent, I'm sure praying, as Sue was interrogated. Dad modeled the character traits of self-control, faith in the justice system, trust in knowing he was doing the right thing.

The judge had no trouble deciding the case. Dad's testimony, the testimony of an eyewitness, and the investigating officer's report were exactly the same. Sue was found guilty and her insurance company was responsible for all the damage. But even more importantly, truthfulness, honesty, self-control, and respect were key factors in the victory.

Lunchbox Note

I am so glad you want the truth to be known. Thanks for standing up for what was right yesterday. I am proud of you!

Training

Recently my twenty-something daughter said to me, "You know, Mom, the other day I was writing a note to one of my friends. I saw her car in the parking lot at the mall and just decided to say hi. I stuck a note in the door handle of her car like you used to do to us. All those years you were writing notes in our lunch, you weren't just telling us we were special. You were teaching us how to encourage others in the same way by your example. I never realized it until the other day!"

Yes, as we write notes and affirm our own children, we are teaching them to do that for others. Through the years, as they are recipients of notes, they learn how much just a few words can mean. Then when they get older and identify a friend or coworker who needs encouragement, they step right in.

What a blessing to watch my children practice this method of encouragement. And sometimes I am the recipient of their notes. I carry a note in my briefcase from my son who was six years old when he wrote it. It says in his very elementary handwriting, "Mom, I love you and I like you. Love, Your Son." I treasure that note and read it often!

Lunchbox Note

I love you and I like you!

A Lunchbox Kid Says

Most of the time my notes just said "Have a good day!" But I always knew they would be there.

—Anna, age 16

Teaching by Example

Teaching by example is extremely important. What we do and how we act gives credibility to the verbal lessons we give our children.

One day I was driving in heavy traffic. Cars were backed up several blocks from the traffic light. That, in turn, had caused cars trying to enter the flow of traffic on this main thoroughfare to be at a standstill. When I arrived at a side street, I paused long enough to allow a car to enter the line. Looking in my rearview mirror, I saw the car behind me do the same thing. I smiled. The driver of that car was my teenage daughter.

Modeling good behavior for our children is not always that easy. But we want our children to grow up to be solid citizens who exhibit good character at all times. Dr. Kirk Neely, pastor and family counselor, says, "The concept of modeling—leading by example—is not a new idea. It is an old idea, tried and true and new in every generation."

How can I instill positive values in my children? How can I live in such a way that my children will mimic the good things I do? What positive (or negative) values do I pass on to my children without even a word?

Before children even talk, they learn to mimic the behavior of those around them. To teach them how to wave goodbye, we wave at them. To teach them how to use a fork and spoon, wash their hands, and put on clothes, we show them by example. Many of the basic lessons in life are learned by imitating someone who has already learned them.

As children get older, we realize that conscious effort will be needed to teach and instill basic principles and values we want to be part of their character. Bit by bit, love note by love note, we are providing the building blocks for the character of our children.

Lunchbox Note (to son)

Last night I noticed you pulled your sister's chair out for her

when she sat down at supper. That was a very thoughtful
thing to do. When you honor and respect others,
it is noticed. I was really proud of you.

———————————————————————

———————————————————————

Lunchbox Note (to daughter)
Last night I heard you knock before you entered your brother's
room. Thank you for respecting his privacy. I am proud of you.

———————————————————————

A Lunchbox Kid Says
I've started leaving notes for my mom and dad
because I know how good it feels to receive one.
—Teal, age 13

Showing Appreciation

Often when we praise our children and try to communicate how special they are to us and how much we appreciate them, they just shrug their shoulders and say, "Aw,
Mom," or "Aw, Dad." When we write it down, it becomes
documented. The love note can become a lifeline when
the child needs a word of encouragement. Examples of
encouraging words are:
• You're a neat kid. I'm glad you are mine.
• I am so proud of you. What a great grade on your test!
• You were so helpful to me last night. Thank you.
• I am seeing what a good example you are for your
younger brothers and sisters. Thank you.

• I was proud to see you helping Mr. Jacobs next door last night. You are such a caring young man.

• The world is a better place because you are in it. Spread lots of your sunshine around today.

• Those cookies you baked for the family last night were delicious. Thank you for sharing your cooking talents.

A Lunchbox Kid Says

On some days my mom might just put a card in there because she wanted to. It's comforting to know that someone loves you and is thinking about you.

—Teal, age 13

Modeling Character

In order to model character to our children, we must act from the overflow of what is deep within us. Somewhere, someone did the same thing for us. We are who we are because of the way character was modeled to us.

Many things contribute to the character of our children. When they are young, they are constantly taught by those around them. Behavior and attitudes on television have a profound impact on helping them to develop their concept of right and wrong. When my children were young, there was a television show they thought was really great to watch. I wouldn't let them watch it because those on the show had attitudes of total disrespect.

Not too long ago, one of my girls came to me and said, "Mom, why wouldn't you let us watch that program? I watched it the other day and I didn't see any violence, sex, or profanity."

"It was their attitudes," I answered. "They were totally disrespectful to authority, the law, and each other."

31

Character has a lot to do with right and wrong. But the character of a person includes the way he or she acts and reacts in the face of adversity. In Paul's letter to the Romans, he reminds us that, "Suffering produces perseverance; and perseverance, character; and character, hope" (Romans 5:3–4). Holding your head high when things are difficult develops understanding, compassion, and strength. Character grown during the hard times is the strongest character of all.

Teaching those most precious to us is an awesome responsibility. But it is a privilege and opportunity to leave a positive character legacy in the lives of our children. However, we must begin to develop that legacy early in their lives! We must constantly be teaching by word and example. Love notes in their lunchboxes are a great way to instill tidbits of character.

An old TV commercial illustrated it this way. A young father and his four-year-old son walked through a field and sat down under a tree. The father reached in his pocket, pulled out a cigarette, and lit up. The son, observing, looked around beside him, picked up a three-and-a-half-inch stick and put it in his mouth. They both began to puff.

Are your kids watching you? All the time. Does it matter what you do, even when you think they are not looking? Absolutely.

Lunchbox Note

*I hope your day is really super and not just so-so!
Learn a lot, flash that gorgeous smile at your teachers,
and tell the gang hi. See you this afternoon. ILY*

Self-Esteem

Every note you write to your child, whether it is a love note, a note of congratulations, or just a joke or riddle for the day, is putting another building block in the foundation of your child's life. Character and self-esteem are not ready-made. They are built layer by layer.

Self-esteem is the way we perceive ourselves. That view is influenced greatly by what we think others think of us. When I was a child we often chanted, "Sticks and stones may break my bones, but words may never hurt me." But the truth of the matter is that words are very important and can inflict life-long wounds. Children are particularly influenced by the words of their parents. If a child grows up in a loving environment, he will be self-assured and confident.

A short word in the lunchbox every day about the value of your child as a person will yield great dividends in the life of your child. Every deposit into the self-esteem bank will multiply.

Lunchbox Note

I believe in you. Reach for the stars!
(This would be a good day for a star sticker or two!)

A Lunchbox Kid Says

The most special note from my mother wasn't in my lunchbox . . . it was in my suitcase when I was traveling on the choir tour one year. She gave me a card a day to read while I was away . . . and this particular day she gave me a card that said that

no one could or would ever love me like she does. I
knew right then and there that if I turned out to
be half the woman my mother was, I was going to be
an awesome woman.

—Kellyn, age 19

Starting the Week Off Right

Sometimes just focusing on a brand new week helps, especially if the week before hasn't been so good. A new start
is always an adventure, a second chance, an opportunity
to do better than the time before. Encourage your child to
face each new week with enthusiasm and a fresh outlook.
Don't carry over the frustrations and disappointments of
the week before.

Mondays at work are often thought of as extra busy,
days to catch up after a weekend off. But for school, the
weekend is a time to not think about schoolwork and have
time off, followed by a brand new day in the educational
process.

So try to make Monday extra special every now and
then. Several suggested Monday love notes are:
• Wasn't the weekend fun? I loved the picnic in the
mountains. I can't picnic with you today, but while you
eat your lunch, you can be sure I am thinking about you.
I hope today is a great day!
• I know last week was kind of a bummer. You felt like you
didn't do well on your test. But this is a new start . . . a different week and I am sure it is going to be a great week for
you. In fact, I hope this is one of the best weeks of your
life!
• I know you were disappointed that your game was
rained out last week. But there is a big game coming up

this week and I know you are going to have a great game. I'll be there cheering for you!

Monday, first day of a new week. Make the most of it.

Lunchbox Fact

The first television-related metal lunchbox was
the Hopalong Cassidy box introduced by Aladdin in 1950.
This box was a great success and launched Aladdin
as one of the leading makers of lunchboxes.

A Lunchbox Kid Says

One Monday morning I was having a bad day. I was ill and my mom made me a nice breakfast to cheer me up, but it did not work! I went to school ill. When lunch came, I opened my lunchbox and there was a note that said, "Hope your day gets better. Love, Mom." That cheered me up. Wow! What a great mom!

—Dustin, age 15

Sharing Daily Events

Sometimes your child's note can be for information. Perhaps there is an impending family event or an afternoon appointment that you don't want your child to forget. A lunchbox reminder to not dawdle on the way out of school may help the afternoon go more smoothly.

If you have a busy day planned at work and will be giving an important presentation, you can include that in the child's note. It will give your child an opportunity to pray for you during the day until you are together again.

Lunchbox Note

I heard you practicing the piano last night.
You are doing so well with your recital piece.
Mrs. Beedy is going to be so surprised this
afternoon when you go for your lesson. Hurry on
out of school so we'll have time for a snack before you go.

It isn't a bad thing for our children to realize that our days are full and that we, too, often have to deal with stresses. Sometimes we have "homework," too! Don't apologize, but realize that dealing with your distractions is good training for their adult life!

Lunchbox Note

Remember the PowerPoint presentation you were helping me
with last night? Today I will be presenting it. Say a prayer for me
right after lunch. Thanks. I know I can always count on you.

Every Day Is an Opportunity

God has given each of us twenty-four hours in every day in which to impact the lives of our children. Don't miss a single minute to love, encourage, instruct, or plant a seed! Many times, there just don't seem to be enough hours in a day. But usually, for me, it not the lack of hours but the misuse of the ones I already have. Some of the things I have tried to remember are:

• Look for the positive things and point them out.

• During the course of the day, if you say five positive

things and one negative thing to your child, the negative will be the one remembered.
• You cannot take back something once it is said.
• Make plenty of time in the day for fun.
• Encourage your child to laugh a lot with you.
• Make respect for one another a priority.
• Often thank God aloud for your child.

Lunchbox Note

You are so thoughtful. Thanks for helping your sister with her homework last night.

A Lunchbox Kid Says

In the eighth grade I got a note from my mom on a day that I had a really hard test. She just said, "Do your best. I love you no matter what! God is with you!" That made me feel special because I realized my mom loves me so much no matter what I do.

—Mollie, age 14

Joint Effort

Packing the lunchbox at our house was always a joint effort. Dad tried to see how much food he could get in that little brown sack and Mom always tried to see just how much love she could put in a few words. Dad's lunches were so good that Andrew once commented, "Jeff has the best lunches in the whole school! Most of us just have a peanut butter and jelly sandwich. But Jeff has turkey on a bagel or leftover chicken with honey mustard sauce or something really good!"

37

Andrew was right. Dad worked very hard to provide something Jeff liked and would enjoy. For a while he was very health conscious, with nothing but meat and celery and carrots in the lunch. Other times tasty cookies and desserts were welcome.

While Dad packed the food, Mom wrote the note. Several friends had called to ask if Mom could include an extra note. She gladly put several extra notes in Jeff's lunch every day. Gregg was one of the extra-note recipients.

One day he was walking through the kitchen. "Mrs. G, as long as you are writing me a note, do you think Mr. G could make me a sandwich, too?"

So lunch preparation every evening became a short order process and Jeff began carrying several extra lunches in his backpack every day! Just another way for us to say to this neat bunch of kids, "We love you!"

Lunchbox Note
You're a neat kid! Have a great day!

A Lunchbox Kid Says
We all waited to see what Jeff had in his lunch!
—Andrew, age 19

Honoring Your Child's Name

Choosing a name for your child takes a lot of thought and prayer. Find a time to share with your child how his or her name was selected. Help your child to feel his or her name is special by creating an acronym in the lunchbox one day.

J — jolly	G — great	K — kind
E — excellent	I — incredible	R — respected
F — fun	N — nice	I — inquisitive
F — fabulous	G — giving	S — solid
	E — exciting	T — truthful
	R — rare	I — imaginative

A good name is more desirable than great riches; to be esteemed is better than silver or gold. Proverbs 22:1

Lunchbox Traditions

Every family has traditions. And the more traditions you have that are distinct to your family, the more special and connected you will feel. The lunchbox can also have traditions of its own.

For our family, the note in itself became a tradition that carried over into many areas of our lives. I know our children were glad to have their lunch because by midday they were hungry. But the first thing they looked for in their lunch was not the food, it was the note!

The lunchbox can become a tradition. Once a lunchbox is carried for a year or two, it doesn't seem right to go off to school without it. When the children were young, they always wanted to include a new lunchbox in the back-to-school shopping. They loved to pick one with their favorite characters on the side and a really nice thermos. As they got older, they liked to see how many years they could carry the same lunchbox. Finally, in high school, they didn't even want a lunchbox! They wanted a brown paper sack so they could throw it away and not have to keep up with it to bring home. And a pliable paper sack was much easier to squash into an already overfull back pack.

For a while, stickers were traditional in the lunchbox. To this day, if you open some of our lunchboxes, you will see stickers stuck here and there. Some of the stickers have conversation bubbles with a message. Some are just "I Love You" stickers. Others reflect the interests of a particular child during that time of life.

During the early lunchbox years, we started providing toothpicks instead of forks to eat with. This was a unique way to eat whatever was in the lunch. It was always awkward to have a piece of chicken or fruit to have to cut at school lunch time. So when our lunchbox fare included a leftover piece of chicken or an apple, we cut it into pieces as we put it in the baggie. Then we made sure there were plenty of toothpicks. As a germ-conscious mom, I always felt like this provided the children a better way of sharing their food without sharing their germs!

If your child is involved in sports, you could start a game day tradition. Purchase a package of napkins that reflect the sport and use them only on game day. Buy some crepe paper or confetti in the team colors and put a little of that in the lunchbox each game day. Even very simple remembrances make lunch a fun and anticipated time and say, "You're special" without any words.

Lunchbox Fact

American Thermos introduced the Roy Rogers lunchbox in 1953 . . . entering the lunch box market full force. This box was nicely lithographed and much more appealing to the eyes of young children. American Thermos was later joined by Aladdin as a major player in the lunchbox market.

Chapter Two

Special Days

First Day of First Grade

I sat in the car and watched my little first-grader run up the steps. Her backpack swayed from side to side, too light to stay down. How heavy could a new pencil and small pad of lined paper be?

She had gotten out of the car almost before the wheels had stopped turning, shouted a quick "Bye, Mom!" over her shoulder, and never looked back.

I, on the other hand, sat in the car with my mouth half open, a big tear threatening to escape one eye, and watched this monumental event in her life. I was only slightly aware that the carpool line now had a big gap where the car in front of me had long ago reached the corner traffic light. The driver behind me was tapping his fingers on the steering wheel, wondering if I was ever going to move. But I was not going anywhere until I saw Kristi safely through the door of the school.

Many thoughts went through my mind. Will the teacher take good care of her? Will she be sensitive to her needs? Will there be nice children in her class? Can she quickly make new friends? What about the schoolwork—will it be too hard for her? Or too easy?

These concerns are probably normal for a mother sending her child off to school for the first time. I discovered some things that made the morning transition from home to school go more smoothly.

Tips to Getting Off to School Smoothly:

• Lay all clothes out at night before going to bed. If your child is independent and needs to feel like the choice of what to wear is hers, put two outfits with all the accessories side by side so she can choose in the morning.

• When finished with homework, gather books and papers and return them to the backpack.

• The night before, make sure any special projects, show and tell, book reports, etc., are by the door.

• Sign papers and read any parent correspondence before you go to bed.

• Pray with your child in the car on the way to school. Don't wait until she has a hand on the door to jump out and join friends.

• And, of course, pack lunch. Be sure to include a note!

Lunchbox Note

*This is a very special day! I know you are going to love school.
Learn a lot and make lots of new friends.
I am proud of my first-grader. I love you very much!*

(*Note:* If your first-grader is not yet reading, stick with a very simple drawn note such as an eye, heart, u or u, r, gr8, or a heart and smiley face!)

First Day of School

It's never fun for summer to come to an end, but it happens every year. Spend as much time as you can with your children during the last few days of summer. Plan a few special activities. Even a shopping trip to buy new notebooks, backpacks, and lunchboxes can be fun. Make an occasion out of it.

One year, a long-awaited movie opened a few days before school started. We decided to make a trip to that movie our last-day-of-summer outing. I suggested each child invite a friend or two, and we packed our van and drove to the movie theater. When I herded our group into the building, the manager looked at me and said, "Did you call for a group rate?"

"No," I replied, "how many do you have to have to make a group?"

"Usually ten," he said. "Looks like you qualify!"

What a nice surprise! And to this day, over ten years later, my children still talk about our group trip to the movies! (Now every time we go to a movie, they want to take a group!)

Lunchbox Note

Wow! I can't believe summer is over and it's time for school again. We had so much fun this summer. Study hard, learn a lot, and let's go get ice cream when you get home!

A Lunchbox kid says

My mom wrote me a note that said, "Have a good first day of school." I was already excited but the note made me really happy.

—Celia, age 10

Labor Day

During the school years of my children, we have gone to school on some holidays and others we've stayed home. Some even vary from year to year. Labor Day is one of those days.

In the years that we had Labor Day off, we have enjoyed a few last family moments of summer playtime. There is something about Labor Day that signals time to get serious about a new school year, even though school has usually been in session for a few weeks in our area.

In the years we have to attend school on Labor Day, it becomes just another school day for the kids. If Dad has the day off, he becomes the chauffeur, experiencing the delights of driving carpool. What often happens is that the children come through the door asking, "Why can't Dad drive carpool all the time?" Invariably, Dad has planned a car game, stopped for ice cream on the way home, or invited a few extra children to join us for the afternoon!

We have a friend, a dad of two, who usually takes his lunch hour so he can be the one to pick up his children every day.

Whoever picks the children up from school will have a treat. They chatter in the car about their day, giving the driver (who usually remains silent) a firsthand glimpse of school life. If your child is not very talkative when he gets in the car after school, try a few open-ended questions to get him going.

• How was school today? If that is answered with simply "fine," ask what was fine! Did you have any tests returned today? What were your grades?

• What did you do at recess? Who did you hang around with?

• What new subjects has Mrs. Strickland started lately?

• What kind of celebration does the school have for Thanksgiving (or any impending holiday)?

Lunchbox Note

Today is a special day to honor all the people in our country who work. The first federal holiday was in 1894. Sorry you had to go to school. I know you work hard, too!

National Citizenship Day (September 17)

This would be another good day to celebrate with a flag in the lunchbox. Specialty stores sell pasta in the shape of flags. A patriotic macaroni salad would be a great conversation starter for the lunch bunch!

If you want to include a little history for your child, remind him this day is to commemorate the signing of our Constitution in 1787. Actually, Citizenship Day was created to combine Constitution Day and I Am an American Day. That happened in 1952 when President Truman signed the day into law.

Lunchbox Note

Guess what? You are a citizen of the United States of America AND a citizen of the Gilden family. You are VERY special!

First Day of Autumn

One of our family traditions is our fall foliage tour. Friends who hear us talk about this day think we are part of a big, organized trip to watch the leaves turn. That is not exactly what happens.

Since our children were very small, in other words for many years now, we have designated one Saturday in October to ride up into the mountains to "see the leaves." But our trip to see the leaves quickly turns into our day to "jump the rocks."

As you begin to get into the mountains, there are many streams with tremendous rocks in and around them. When the children were little, we used to picnic on the rocks. As they got older and braver, they would ask if they could go jump on the rocks. The only rule was that I must be able to see them from where I sit on a big rock in the sun.

One year we had a young friend from India with us. She had spent years in India with rock jumping as one of her primary sources of entertainment. When she saw the rocks, her eyes lit up.

"This is just like in India," she squealed. "Oh, Mom, can I go jump on the rocks? Please?"

I was glad for Kim to jump on the rocks but forgot to tell her the one rule. Kim quickly sailed through the air from one rock to another and disappeared from sight. I had no idea that jumping on the rocks in India was without rules or boundaries.

The entire family sprang into action, running along the bank to try to catch up with Kim. When we finally found her, she was all smiles.

"This is so much fun," she said.

"But," I said, "you can't go running off. You have to stay where we can see you!"

"Sorry, sorry," Kim said. But the smile on her face let us know that the pleasure had been worth my fussing!

First Day of Autumn Lunchbox Note
This is the first day of autumn. You know what
that means . . . shorter days, cooler weather, basketball season
is right around the corner, the leaves are turning. I can't wait
to go on our annual fall foliage trip. What a fun time!

After a Hard Homework Day

Fifth grade homework. At our elementary school, fifth grade is the dreaded year. There is so much to learn and the focus has shifted from helping your student learn the alphabet and the basics of math to concentrating on writing skills and making sure the student is ready for middle school.

When I attended fifth grade PTO for the first time, I knew our homework habits were going to have to change. No longer could we linger over snacks and play guessing games about "What happened at school today?" The teacher said some homework days would require several hours of work.

That proved to be true, so I tried to structure the afternoons to include a short period of exercise and free time and time to finish homework before supper. I found that if I took a snack to eat in the car, blood sugar levels would be in good shape and the children often got a second wind before we got home!

Some good snacks to take in the car are:
• Juice boxes
• Bottles of water
• Fruit

- Cereal or granola bars
- Homemade cookies (always welcome!)

Lunchbox Note

Wish I could have been more help with your math homework
last night. We didn't learn it that way in the good ol' days.
Be sure to ask your teacher for a little extra help if you still need it.
Remember 1+1+1+1= (Dad+Mom+Sis+you) = our family
and it's the perfect answer!

Birthdays

One year my daughter's birthday fell on the day of the annual spring festival at school. The only thing she asked for that year was a turn in the "dunking booth" at the carnival. After talking to the principal, the logistics were finally worked out and she got her wish. That birthday is still a highlight year!

Most older students can't decide if they want a birthday party or not! When in doubt you can always organize a surprise celebration, then the student doesn't have to make the decision about whether or not to have a party!

It doesn't have to be fancy; a gathering place, some light refreshments, and festive mood are all that is necessary. But if you don't want to do the party thing, there are still ways that you can help make the day special.

Take advantage of local media to help say "Happy Birthday." If there is a radio station that your student listens to frequently or at a certain time of the day, call and ask that they wish her a happy birthday. Some television stations take time for birthday wishes on the morning shows. Include the birthday in church or neighborhood newsletters.

One of the most fun "mailboxes" to use is your student's car. Before school is dismissed, take your extra key and fill the car with balloons. Tie a few balloons to the antenna. If balloons are not your style, stretch a birthday banner across the front seat. Or have a special gift in the driver's seat when school is dismissed.

Lunchbox Note

Happy Birthday! May you have many more wonderful birthdays! I am so proud of you. (You may be able to find a small music box that plays happy birthday. Or make a card to use for the basis of your note.)

A Lunchbox Kid says

Mom always puts something simple in my lunchbox. It always makes me feel good that she sends stuff for me to read. On my birthday, she usually brings my lunch to school.

—Lawton, age 13

Firstborn's Birthday

Very few things equal the thrill of becoming a parent. Remembering the birth of your first child always brings a warm feeling inside. At your first child's birth, your life was changed forever, right?

One way to make your firstborn feel special on the anniversary of that event is to emphasize how special her birthday is for you as a parent. Take time to point out

49

several things that are different in your life since the day she was born. For example:

• "My sleeping pattern was changed for life. But those waking hours sure are fun." (Sometimes there are just too many of them!)

• "I never knew it took so long to walk to the end of the driveway to get the mail. You used to pick up every stick, leaf, and stone. We explored all kinds of things together."

• "You asked me why I usually finish dinner before you do. When you were born, I learned to finish mine as soon as possible because as soon as you finished yours, I couldn't sit at the table any longer."

• "I never knew how much fun it was to read to someone else."

• "Thanks for showing me how to make a game out of so many things. Life has been so much more fun since you were born."

Lunchbox Note

Ten years ago you made me a mother.
Thank you. What an honor it is to be your mom!
I thank God for you every day.

Middle Child's Birthday

"It's not fair!" wailed our middle child . . . again.

Many middle children spend a lot of time and energy feeling that things would be different if only they had been born at another time in the family. In *The Birth Order Book, Why You Are the Way You Are*, Kevin Leman describes middle children as "born *too late* to get the privileges and

special treatment the firstborn seemed to inherit by right
. . . born *too soon* to strike the bonanza that many lastborns
enjoy—the relaxing of the disciplinary reins."

With a little special attention to the plight of the middle
child, that spot in the family can be a very cozy place.

1. Remember that with the arrival of child number three,
the status of the second child abruptly changed from baby
to middle. Suddenly, she must compete for attention. Plan
a special time each day to spend with the middle child.
2. A middle child wants to be more and more independent. She may feel overshadowed at times. The older sibling always seems to do it better. The younger sibling
needs and gets more help. Look for opportunities to focus
on her. Invite her to accompany you on short errands.
3. Develop close communication skills. Even if the conversations don't seem meaningful, it is important to have
one-on-one talking time with your middle child. Listen
intently.
4. A frequent complaint of older middle children is that
their formative years are obviously lacking in the family
photo album. Start now. Take plenty of pictures of your
middle child. A birthday picture each year would be a
good start.
5. Pray out loud with your child. Let her hear you asking
God to bless her by name. Acknowledge that she has special
needs (as do each of your children). Share your confidence
that God can meet those needs.

Every child is special and needs individual attention. No
matter what the birth order, encourage your child to
develop positive characteristics and cope with negative
aspects of her personality.

Birthdays are especially important to the middle child. Some of them feel it is their only day of the year in the spotlight. Make a big "to do" over your middle child's birthday. If your schedule allows, eat lunch at school with your middle child on her birthday. Have a balloon in the car when you pick up at school. Hang a banner in the birthday person's bedroom. Celebrate, celebrate, celebrate!

And, don't forget, lots of hugs regardless of birth order!

Lunchbox Note

Happy Birthday to my special middle child! You are surrounded by love from the top and the bottom. God put you in a very wonderful place in our family. That is so cool! I hope today is fun. We'll celebrate when you get home!

Youngest Child's Birthday

When the "baby" has a birthday, the whole family gets into the act at our house. No matter which of his birthdays we are celebrating, his big sisters are always wonderful helpers.

When he was young, they directed games and made balloon animals to entertain his friends. As he got older, the celebrations became more sophisticated and grown-up. But no matter what his age or stage, the birthday has been an occasion to remember!

The lunchbox can be a continuation of the day-long celebration. Include a special card. Use balloon stickers to "decorate" the lunchbox. Put a cupcake in for dessert that has the appropriate number of candles.

If your school allows, have a school party. It doesn't have to be elaborate. Just one of your child's favorite snacks for the whole class to enjoy is sufficient. When my son was five, he wanted to have a school party and serve cereal and milk. The teacher said that no one had ever brought cereal and milk before! But the kids loved it and asked for seconds. And I didn't feel like I had fed them something too sweet or unhealthy!

Don't forget the home party, too! It may be as simple as the immediate family gathered around the table with a cake. Or you can invite the neighborhood, the cousins, or some special friends!

Lunchbox Note

Happy Birthday! This is your special day.
Our family was complete on this day six years ago
when you were born! You are special.

Happy Birthday, Daughter!

When our second daughter was born, I was thrilled. I already had one daughter and I knew what fun a little girl was. So I was excited to have another girl to love and do girlie things with!

Unthinking people still said to me, "Well, I guess you would like to have a little boy." And I remember thinking to myself, *Do people really do that? Do they really have more and more babies for gender reasons?*

I was thrilled at the birth of my firstborn daughter. Becoming a mother was an incredible moment! She completed a part of me that I never fully knew was there. I never imagined how great the blessing of a child could be. I was in uncharted territory.

But I think the second time, the thrill was there because I *knew* how much a daughter meant to me. I was in familiar territory and delighted to go there again. Pink could continue to be a popular color at our house!

Lunchbox Note

*I will never forget the thrill of holding you in my arms
for the first time all those years ago. Today is a special day
for me, too. Happy Birthday to my sweet daughter.*

Happy Birthday, Son!

After two girls, people assumed during pregnancy number three, I was still hoping for a boy. To be totally honest, I loved having girls. I was primed to continue with pink. In fact, I had always wanted four girls. For some reason, as I was growing up four girls had seemed the perfect number of children.

But God had other plans. I never even considered that number three would be a boy. But in the delivery room when the doctor looked at precious child number three, he said, "You have a son!"

A son? I don't think anyone was more shocked than I was. We were all set up for girls and I just assumed we'd be one girl closer to our four girls! But I was wrong. And I would have missed so much if I had been allowed to choose the sex of my children. I would have missed so much if I had never had a son.

Jeff was special from the moment I saw him. And the way he looked at me was different. My girls loved me and we had a great time together. I was looking forward to many years of wonderful girl stuff. But the first time Jeff looked at me, I knew he loved me in a different way. I can't really explain it, but it was different and deep. Yes, he was only an infant when he gave me that first look, but when he lay in my arms and our eyes connected . . . wow!

That bond continues today. Just the way he says "Mom" can send my heart leaping and a prayer of thanksgiving soaring up to the Father for this child who has blessed me so.

So on the birthday of your son, make sure he understands the depth of your love for him. Let him know that he has blessed your life. What a special day for you both.

Sons are a heritage from the Lord, children a reward from him. Psalm 127:3

Lunchbox Note

Happy Birthday, Son! It was a special day for me when you were born. Can't wait to eat cake this afternoon!

After the Birthday

After three children, it was not always easy to be creative and come up with an unusual theme for birthday parties. But this one had been easy.

Jeff loved to go to his grandfather's farm to fish. So this birthday party was going to be a fishing trip to the farm. It was Jeff's tenth birthday. As was our custom, he had invited ten friends. (The rule at our house was that you could invite the same number of guests as your age.)

The day came and we loaded our van with excited young men. Most were city boys who had not had much fishing experience. In preparation my husband gathered fishing poles, purchased hundreds of crickets, bought enough stringers so each boy could have his own, and enlisted our teenagers and their friends to help bait hooks, take fish off hooks, and generally help the boys practice safe fishing habits.

Papoo, Jeff's grandfather, stocked his pond and fed and fertilized the fish regularly so this maiden experience would be one to remember!

When the van stopped, the doors were opened wide and ten excited boys flew out.

"Where do we fish, Papoo?" one asked.

"Where can I catch a big fish?" asked another.

"Show me where they are biting best," begged another boy.

We quickly paired the boys with a teenage helper, distributed poles and crickets, and pointed them toward the pond. Papoo spread them out around the pond so there was no chance of anyone hooking another ten-year-old.

Hooks had not been in the water long when Ben let out a yell. "I've got one. Ooo, he's big. I hope I can land him." Nine little boys immediately swarmed around Ben.

"Ben's got one!"

"Hang on, Ben, you can reel him in."

"Wow! That fish must be a monster!"

Ben pulled and wound and tugged and rocked his reel from side to side and finally pulled in a beautiful four-pound bass. The swarm continued to wiggle with excitement. No one could believe that they had just started fishing and already one person had landed a whopper!

"I'm going to get him mounted," Ben said proudly.

"I'll let you and your mom decide that," I said. "OK, boys, let's get back to fishing."

Slowly the swarm went back to their fishing poles. But one by one, they looked around to see where Ben was fishing. And one by one, they moved over to join him!

Next Day Lunchbox Note

(This would be a good day to include some fish crackers or gummi worms in the lunchbox!) What a fun birthday party! I think all your friends enjoyed fishing at Papoo's farm. Everyone wanted to go where Ben was once he caught that big fish, didn't they? You will have a lot of chances in life to follow others. Just make sure what they are doing isn't leading you astray!

National Popcorn Popping Month

October is National Popcorn Popping Month. Several times this month include a popcorn snack or dessert or promise to have a popcorn snack when you get home. Or, if your child really likes surprises, when you finish putting the lunch items in the lunchbox, fill every leftover spot with popcorn. When he opens the lunchbox, what an unexpected sight!

January also lists a Popcorn Day. It's easy to find special days on the calendar to tie in to your lunchbox themes. You can also do an online search for special calendar days.

At your local library, you can also find books on the subject of calendar days. *Celebrate Today! More Than 4,000 Holidays, Celebrations, Origins, and Anniversaries* by John Kremer (Prima Publishing, 1996). *Kids Celebrate! Activities for Special Days Throughout the Year* by Marie Bonfanti

Esche, Clare Bonfanti Braham, and Mary Jones (illustrator) (Chicago Review Press, 1998).

Lunchbox Note

This is National Popcorn Popping Month.
Did you guess?

First Day of Winter

Winter is a favorite time at our house, especially when it snows. In our area of the country snow usually falls only once a year so it is a very special time.

One year I had to be away on business during January and, wouldn't you know it, we had a great snow. When I called home, the children were so excited. I was excited for them but disappointed that I was missing all the fun.

When I returned home, the children met me at the door. "We have a surprise for you!" They all were jumping up and down so I knew it must be a really good surprise.

"Close your eyes and hold out your hands," Jeff said.

Soon I felt something cold and hard and round in my hand.

"Look," he said. "We saved you a snowball."

"What a thoughtful thing to do!" I exclaimed.

"Wanna have a snowball fight?" he asked.

I found several more snowballs carefully wrapped in tin foil and stored in the freezer. I left them there the rest of the winter, a precious reminder of the love of my children. What a treasure that they wanted me to be a part of their winter fun.

Lunchbox Note
Winter's here, winter's here.
Do you think we'll have some snow this year?

Veteran's Day

Veteran's Day would be a great day to include a few flags in the lunch. Or if the day's menu includes a sandwich on white bread, dip a toothpick in blue food coloring to make a box and red coloring for stripes and create a flag on the top of the sandwich. This could spark a lot of discussion with the lunch bunch! Your child could even let them guess why their sandwich is a flag!

Lunchbox Note

Grandpa fought in the war so we could be free.
He was so proud of his service. You'll see
lots of flags today celebrating Veteran's Day.
Have a great one!

Test Day

I held another flash card up. It read "6 x 6." It seemed like we had been studying the multiplication tables for a very long time. But I also knew this basic stuff was really important to learn. And the only way to do that was to memorize it.

"OK," I said. "Do you remember this one?"

"30?" The question in my child's voice was evident.

59

"That's close," I said.

We had been at this for a while and had to master the sixes for tomorrow's test. I thought of games to play and made up rhymes. Anything that was a little catchy seemed to help.

Finally, we were finished and able to go to bed.

Sometimes it takes a little extra help to get these basic skills. We just need to remember that's what they are—basic. And it is vitally important that our children have a good foundation to build their education on.

Their spiritual education is that way, too. Little by little we must lay the foundation for their relationship with God. Little by little, love note by love note, you have the opportunity to lay that foundation. When our children see us in a close relationship with our Heavenly Father, they begin to desire that same kind of closeness. As parents we are modeling for our children what it means to be a Christian. Remember that everything they see you do is sending a message and becoming part of their foundation.

Lunchbox Note

You really studied hard last night.
I know you will do your best. I am so proud of you.

A Lunchbox Kid says

My mom left me a note in my lunchbox when I was in the seventh grade. It said, "Hope you have a great day and I hope you pass your math quiz." I love my mom and I know she loves me, too. I'm glad to know

when I go home, I have a great mom to go to. That
note was several years ago and I still remember it.
—Dustin, age 15

National Thank You Month

It is fun to find a month that can help you reinforce positive behavior. January is one of those months because it
is National Thank You Month.

Having to remind your child to say "please" and "thank"
you occurs too frequently in many families. But when we can
find a reason to be conscious of doing it, such as National
Thank You Month, it becomes almost like a game.

Challenge your child to see how many times he can
say thank you to someone each day in January. Help your
child to think of people who are often overlooked when it
comes to saying thank you, such as the school cafeteria
personnel, bus drivers, crossing guards, mail carriers,
garbage collectors, and newspaper carrier. Provide paper
and colorful pens so he can write a short note to some of
these folks expressing appreciation.

Make a point chart at home and challenge the entire
family to say special thank-you's this month. Award one
point for each remembered thank-you. At the end of the
month cook a special meal for the person with the most
points.

Lunchbox Note

*Since January is National Thank You Month,
I am going to try to remember to say thank you each day in
your lunch. First of all, thank God that you have some lunch!*

Other January thank-you suggestions:
• Thank you for taking out the garbage last night.
• Thank you for helping your sister with her homework last night.
• Thank you for your wonderful smile. It always cheers me up!
• Thank you for cooperating with your dad at the soccer field.
• Thank you for being a special child!
• Thank you for raking Grandma's yard for her. I think you are her favorite grandson!
• Thank you for sharing the cookies you made with the Wilsons next door. I know they miss having homemade cookies since their girls aren't at home to bake any more.
• Thank you for your laughter. I love to hear it!

Valentine's Day

Take advantage of all the "conversation stuff" available this week. You may want to buy some extra for days you don't have time to write a note.

Boxes of conversation hearts can be used as the note. Pick one or two hearts with a message that is appropriate for your child. Sometimes several can be combined to make a longer message. If your child regularly eats lunch with the same group, pick out a heart for each of the group. They will really appreciate the extra thought.

Lunchbox Note

Will you be my Valentine today? Out of your whole class I pick you! You stole my heart the minute I saw you!

A Lunchbox kid says

I carried my lunch to school in a paper bag. My mother wrote notes on the outside of the lunch bags—sometimes it was Scripture, sometimes she drew stick figures of my mom and dad at home with my little sister.

I remember one Valentine's Day Mom put a special gift in my lunch. I was in the 10th grade, and I felt really special. When my friends saw that I had received a special gift in my lunch, their jaws dropped! They were really impressed.

—Dawn, age 35

Countdown to an Event

Lunchboxes are a great way to help kids keep up with time. When your child is anxious for a special day to come, a reminder at lunch is a nice way for him or her to keep up with the days.

There are a few things to remember, however, when you are using this method of "calendaring."

Don't start too early. The counting will get old if it is allowed to drag on and on!

Young children can be reminded with objects to count. For example, ten days before your child's birthday, include a baggie with ten pieces of small chocolate candy. On this first day, tell your child that when there is only one piece left in the bag, the next day will be his birthday. Just don't forget to include the baggie each day. It will be the first thing your child looks for when the lunchbox is opened!

For older children, you may use only the written numbers as you look forward to an event.

Christmas or spring vacation is an eagerly awaited break from the routine. Buy a roll of sugar cookies, cut into the shape of numbers and bake them. Then include the numbers in descending order as you count down to the holidays. If you are counting to the Christmas holidays, you could just use the sugar cookie roll that has Christmas trees in the middle of a sugar cookie and write the numbers on the tree before baking. Use an egg yolk mixed with food coloring to "paint" the numbers on the cookies.

Use small stickers on the inside of the lunchbox lid. Remove one each day. When the day arrives, put a sticker in the same location that says, "Happy Birthday, Vacation Begins Tomorrow," or whatever the occasion.

Day Before a School Holiday

Students often begin vacation mentally before the final school bell has rung! Teachers often struggle with those last few hours before a long break. Encourage your student to anticipate the coming vacation but to remember that school is still a priority until that bell rings.

If you are going to do something special as a family, involve the children in the planning but don't overdo. The more you talk about the upcoming family event, the more your child will want to put aside school work and start celebrating!

With younger children, sit down and take a look at the school work that must be done before the holiday. Help your child to make a plan so that all work will get done before the last day. Implementing a plan will help your child develop good organizational skills.

For older children, a simple reminder not to procrastinate will have to do. Make sure you don't cross over into the nagging category.

Lunchbox Note

Today should be a breeze and then you get a few days off.
That will be a treat! Looking forward
to having you home for a few days.

St. Patrick's Day (March 17)

When we think of St. Patrick's Day, we immediately think green! In fact, tradition has it that if you don't wear green, you may get pinched!

St. Patrick's Day originated in Ireland to commemorate the day that St. Patrick died. This day was set aside as a religious holiday, a day to pray for missionaries around the world. In our country, we tend to think leprechauns, shamrocks, good luck, and green. Some cities even go so far as to dye rivers green.

This should definitely be a green lunch day! And don't forget to write your love note on green paper.

Lunchbox Note

I hope you wore green today so you won't get pinched! If you
didn't, just carry this note with you and let it stick out of your
pocket. That way you will have some green! You are my favorite
boy/girl in the lunchroom no matter what color you are wearing.

First Day of Spring

In our area of the country, the daffodils poke their little green heads up before we have put away our winter coats.

Occasionally, they can even be seen sticking up through the snow! But once the "daffydils" are spotted, we know spring is just around the corner.

Along with the extended hours of sunshine, the budding of the trees, and the reawakening of the flower garden, comes spring fever. And the kids are not the only ones who suffer from this annual malady!

Plan something fun for the afternoon of the first few days of spring. Instead of going home, pack a picnic snack and drive to the neighborhood park. After snack announce that you are going to do homework in the park instead of the house that day. Or you can do the same thing in your back yard. Allow a play break to enjoy the advent of spring after a session of homework.

Take a walk around your neighborhood noticing all the new life that is emerging. Comment on the changes in nature that occur in spring.

This would be a great time to talk about God's plan of salvation. God planned for us to get rid of our old habits that don't please Him and become fresh and new by asking for His forgiveness. God can make every day like springtime in our lives if we live our days for Him. But that can't happen unless we ask Him to be a part of our lives and ask for His forgiveness. If you compare springtime to salvation, be sure your child is old enough to process and understand the comparison.

Find a pretty quiet spot on a rock or bench and talk to your child about God's plan. Make sure he understands how much God loves him. He loves us all so much that His Son, Jesus, died for us.

Recently a friend was telling a five-year-old about Jesus. My friend very simply stated that Jesus died for his sins. She explained to this energetic little boy how much

God loved him. "All you have to do to live with Jesus forever in heaven is to tell God you are sorry for your sins and ask Jesus to come into your heart."

"That's it?" he asked.

"Yes," she nodded. "That's it!"

Sometimes we try to make things too complicated. Share your relationship with God with your child at every opportunity. The words don't have eloquent . . . just heartfelt!

Lunchbox Note

Spring has sprung! Let's enjoy!
(Of course, I love you in every season!)

Day Before a Game

We can't do anything about the outcome of our child's sporting event. However, we can do our best to make sure the child knows that no matter what the end result of the game, you are still the parent of a winner.

1. Always affirm your child.

2. Avoid tying winning to having fun. Fun should come from your child's enjoyment of the sport and competition, not from winning.

3. Engage your child in conversation after the game by asking questions like:

"So what did you learn from today's game? Can it help make you a better player tomorrow?"

4. Use your conversations to take advantage of teachable moments. Say things like: "Life is going to present you opportunities to grow, like mistakes made in a ball game.

It is important to take advantage of those opportunities and apply the lessons you learn so you are better prepared the next time around."

5. Relieve your child of the pressure to win. Help him feel he has made a significant contribution to your life.

6. Enjoy your child's participation in sports, knowing that regardless of the outcome of the competition, your child is a winner!

Lunchbox Note

You are the best goalie the Redbirds ever had. I will be there to watch you play. No matter what the score, you are a winner with me!

Day After a Game

According to a "Youth Sports In America" study, over 30 million children participate annually in organized sports.

Game day can often be stressful. Not only is there the pressure to win, but also by the time they get to the game, children may have had to search for a lost shin guard, help Mom get snacks together for the team, or wait for a family member to get there at the last minute. How can we help make game day a special occasion and a positive experience?

Every time your child steps into the sporting environment, there is the opportunity for losing, having a bad game, or getting hurt feelings. Whether your child is a star or has never played before, it is important to avoid tying success to victory during competition.

Shane McKenzie, vice president of Partnership for Upward Unlimited, a national sports ministry, asserts,

"Success is found in your child giving 100 percent of his or her effort." No matter what the score of a game, make sure your child knows that he or she is a winner!

Lunchbox Note

*Great game on Saturday! You gave it all you had,
and I was so proud of you! Go Panthers (team name)!*

A Lunchbox Kid says

My dad always cheers me on at my games. After one game he wrote me a note that said, "I love you, man! Great job last night. You had some great swish shots. Keep up the good work!"

—Jacob, age 12

Red Rover

"Red rover, red rover, send Linda right over!" One of my favorite recess games at school was Red Rover. To play, you divide into two teams. It doesn't matter how large or how small the teams are as long as each side has three or more players.

All the children on a team hold hands to form a human chain. They call out a friend's name on the opposite team to be "sent over." The chosen one runs as fast as possible to try to break through the chain. If the defenders drop hands, the one who has come over chooses a person to take back to his team with him. If the defense holds, the challenger becomes a member of that team.

The excitement and anticipation of waiting to hear whose name would be called was tremendous. I remember the thrill of hearing my name called and being chosen to represent my team.

But even greater is the thrill that comes in knowing that for the game that really matters, everyday life, my name has already been called. I don't have to wait and see if it is my turn. God has called each one of us by name to come to Him. We need only to respond to His calling to be one of the chosen.

Lunchbox Note

*I am so glad God chose you to be my son/daughter.
I know it is up to Him. But if He had lined up
all the children in the world and let me choose one,
I would have picked you!*

A Lunchbox Kid says

When I was in 8th grade, I got a "lunchbox note" from my mom . . . it was a red heart shaped card and on the front it said, "I love you! Love, Mom." I've always known that my mom loves me, but after a hard day, just to get a note that said "I love you" from my mom made my day and brought a smile to my face! In fact, I'm in 11th grade, and to this day, I have that same note!

—Lauren, age 17

Friend Day

We live in a neighborhood without children, so one of the highlights of the week for my children was always "Friend Day." They loved to have friends come home from school to play. Sometimes the biggest quandary on my part was how to entertain our young guests!

For Girls:

• Provide clothes, shoes, and pocketbooks for a dress-up session.

• Buy a tub of ready-made cookie dough so they can make cookies with a minimum of supervision. Let them decide the size and shape of the cookies.

For Boys:

• Give them a magnifying glass (unbreakable) and challenge them to find the best bug in the yard.

• Have two equal sets of materials and let them have a building contest. Any materials will do—marshmallows and toothpicks, locking blocks, graham or saltine crackers, playing cards. Food items are fun because you can provide extras just for eating!

Lunchbox Note

*I am so glad Reggie is coming home
from school with you. Can't wait!*

Going Home with a Friend Day

When your child is invited to go home from school with a friend, you may find yourself with a free afternoon. When this happens for the first time, you don't quite know what to do with yourself. An entire afternoon without kids, snacks, and homework may even make you feel a little lost.

But you shouldn't feel that way. Keep in mind that your child is on an adventure. He is having a great time exploring a new environment. He is seeing how other families do things and interact with one another. He may come home with some new ideas for your family to try. Or he may come home with a new appreciation for your family and the security he feels in knowing just how things are always done.

Just in case you don't know what to do with yourself when your child is away for the afternoon, here are a few suggestions.

• Plan a shopping trip with a friend. Include a leisurely lunch and plan to look in shops that you don't visit when you have the children along!

• Do only the essential errands. Then pamper yourself with a hot bath and a good book!

• Invite your husband to take a few hours off to do something special with you.

• Visit a friend you have been meaning to visit but just haven't found the time.

• Do an adult craft that you put off trying because time didn't allow.

• Cook a really nice dinner.

• Enjoy being with yourself! The first few times I had this experience, I wandered around for a while trying to decide what I could do. When the children were home, I spent time wishing I could have just a few hours of solitude. Now that the dreamed-of solitude had presented itself, I couldn't decide what to do with it! It didn't take me too long to get over those feelings!

Lunchbox Note

Have a great time at Adam's house. Isn't it great to have such a good friend? See you when I pick you up!

American Bike Month (May)

Look for special monthly celebrations that the whole family can be involved in. May, American Bike Month, is one of those.

Plan special family bike outings. You may want to ask another family to join you on a nature trail ride/picnic. Enjoy the beautiful weather. Plan several things you would like to do together as a family when school is out for the year.

Lunchbox Note

Let's take a bike hike when you get home!

Last Day of School

Parents and students are always ready to let out a big sigh on the last day of school. Another year is complete and summer looks like a long time of fun and family time.

This is a time to reflect on the good things about this school year. How has your child matured? What specific things has he learned, not just from the books but about life? Now that the pressure of report cards is over for the year, compliment your child on all the accomplishments of the year. Point out specific times that you were proud of how a challenge was met.

Look forward to the summer. Make a list of fun things to do as a family and start right away to check things off the list. Summer goes by so quickly that a little planning helps to make the most of the time available.

Lunchbox Note

Whew! You made it to the last day. I am so proud of you. Enjoy your lunch—tomorrow we can eat together! I love you.

Chapter Three

Christmas in the Lunchbox

December Notes

Before first report cards of the year are issued, commercial establishments begin to display lighted trees, greenery, Santa Claus, and tinsel. Some people feel the need to skip straight from summer to Christmas to stay ahead of the stores. You find yourself competing with the glitz of retailers as you try to help your children focus on what is really important during the month of December. I suppose if we were to take a survey of all the children in one class at school, we would receive varied answers about what Christmas really is— Jesus' birthday, Santa Claus, presents, trees, lights, and the list would probably go on. But whatever the answer, a child's response to that question will certainly come from the way his or her family celebrates the holidays.

Many families gather around the table each week to celebrate Advent, anticipating the coming of the birth of the Savior. But whether or not your family practices that tradition, many more opportunities exist to help our children prepare their hearts to worship the babe in the manger. We can even use the lunchbox to help our children prepare for a worshipful Christmas season. If you are short on time and your creativity is already maxed out for the season, try using a few of the ideas in this section to make your child's holiday lunchbox more festive.

Deck the Lunchbox

Many stickers, whistles, pencils, candy, and other novelties are available during the month of December. Look for quick ways to decorate your notes, stickers to stick on sandwich bags, and novelties to direct your child's attention to the true meaning of the season.

Buy a pack of Christmas napkins to include each day. Better yet, look in the drawer for leftover napkins from last year's parties. It is likely you will never have another occasion to use them. Use them to color your child's day.

Sandwich bag companies have also gotten into the Christmas spirit and you can now buy sandwich bags with preprinted holiday motifs. Keep a box on hand and you will not have to do anything additional to the lunch to give it a festive feel.

Attach a "countdown to the holidays" calendar to the top of the lunchbox. That will help your child realize that progress is being made toward the days of vacation. Some local newspapers have a "Countdown 'til Christmas" box. You could simply cut that out each morning and tape it to the inside top of the box. Or create your own countdown calendar inside the lid. Include a small calendar where your child can mark off the days with a pencil. Or create the calendar with individual squares of paper for each day and he can remove the day's block as it passes.

If you want to create a lunchbox surprise that the whole lunch bunch will be talking about, decorate the inside of the lunchbox for the holidays. A little leftover garland from a home project and a few red bows will make the lunch festive and bring a smile to your child's face. Don't go over board. Just a little greenery (artificial, of course) around the perimeter of the box will work. Or twist greenery or a green pipe cleaner into a small circle, add a bow and you will have a "wreath" to secure to the inside of the box!

A Lunchbox kid says

One Christmas all I asked for was my own phone. When I told my mom what I wanted she didn't say much so I wasn't even sure if she heard me. It didn't look good for getting my wish! In my lunchbox one day I got a note from Mom. It said:

> Have a great day. Won't be long 'til Christmas.
> Love, Mom
> PS Hint 2354

I didn't know what that meant. But when I got home from school that day, I went to my room and put my backpack on the bed. All of a sudden I heard a phone ring . . . somewhere in my room.

I searched and finally found a brand new phone under the dresser. And the number was 555-2354!

—Jamie, age 18

Weekly Christmas Notes

For your lunchbox notes, you may choose a plan that includes focusing on a certain theme each week. That is also a meaningful way to celebrate and help your child stay focused on the real meaning of the season.

Week One

• *Monday Note:* This is a really busy time of the year, isn't it? Don't you love all the bright lights? When you see all the lights, remember Jesus is the light of the world. Do you have a friend at school who needs to know about the light of the world?

• *Tuesday Note:* Thanks for helping me put the wreath on the door. It really looks pretty! When we look at our beautiful wreath, a circle of green, let's remember that God's love is never ending.

• *Wednesday Note:* The candles in the windows really shine at night. With one in every window, they light up the whole house. When we see candles, remember that your light, no matter how small, can make a difference.

• *Thursday Note:* The picture you drew of a Christmas tree looked just like our tree. I'm going to hang it on the refrigerator. Every time you look at our tree, remember that Jesus loves you so much He died for you. He hung on a cross made out of a tree.

• *Friday Note:* Someone put a very interesting present under the tree when I wasn't looking. Was that you? When you look under our tree and you see all the presents, think about Jesus. He was God's gift to us. He gave Jesus to us because He loved us so much.

Week Two

• *Monday Note:* I am really looking forward to coming to your Christmas program at school. You will be my favorite singer out of all the others! We'll be singing Christmas carols a lot this month. When you sing, remember it is always important to make a joyful noise unto the Lord. You can do that at Christmas and all year long!

• *Tuesday Note:* You have been really working hard lately. I am so proud of the way you are earning money to buy Christmas presents for a child whose family doesn't have as much as we do. That is very special. Christmas is a good time to do that. But remember, we can help others any time of the year.

• *Wednesday Note:* Candy canes are good, aren't they? Every time you see one, think of the crooks that the shepherds carried to catch a wandering sheep. Remember, God keeps His eye on us just like the shepherd watches his sheep.

• *Thursday Note:* I went shopping yesterday and couldn't decide what to give Aunt Lou for Christmas. God knew just what to give us for Christmas, didn't He? He knew we needed Jesus.

• *Friday Note:* I found a new recipe I thought I would try for Christmas dinner. When we sit down to Christmas dinner, I hope we all remember Jesus is the bread of life.

Week Three
This focus of this week's notes will be the manger and the figures visiting the baby Jesus. The weekend before you begin this series would be a good time to get the manger scene out of the box and have a special family time of putting it together.

• *Monday Note:* You did such a good job of placing the stable on the piano last night. Do you ever wonder how the innkeeper must have felt when he got the place ready for baby Jesus to be born? Do you think he knew what he was doing was really important?

• *Tuesday Note:* Mary, Joseph, and Baby Jesus are the center of attention in our nativity scene. That's the way it should be. We should all keep our eyes on Jesus, not just at Christmas but all the time.

• *Wednesday Note:* The shepherds traveled a long way to see Jesus, didn't they? You know which one is my favorite shepherd? The one who is holding his head. I think he has a headache. Wonder why?

• *Thursday Note:* The angel on the top of our nativity scene looks like she is really watching over everyone, doesn't she? That was her assignment from God. I believe God's angels watch over us every day.

• *Friday Note:* When you get home today, look at all the figures in the nativity scene. They are all coming to see Jesus. Most of them traveled a long way to get to see Him. Aren't we glad Jesus is always right here with us and we don't have to travel and look for Him?

Just because school gets out for vacation, you don't have to stop writing notes. Continue with daily reminders left on the counter when you go to work or on your child's pillow at night. You will be spending more time together during the holidays and can verbally remind her how special this season is. However, when you talk, try to help your child remember that Jesus' love is not just for a season. It is for all year long!

Thanks be to God for his indescribable gift! 2 Corinthians 9:15

Advent Focus

If you don't have an advent wreath for your home, you may want to start a new tradition this year and add an advent wreath to your holiday décor. An advent wreath in the center of your dining table and the appropriately lit candles will reinforce the tidbits of the advent celebration you are able to include in your child's lunchbox. Frequent mention of the true meaning of the season and strategically placed visual reminders will keep your child's thoughts on Jesus and the miracle of His birth.

You may want to designate Monday of each week as your advent focus. Each December Monday begin your note with "This week we will celebrate . . .

First Week of Advent (This may start in the latter days of November depending on year's calendar.)

This is the week we will celebrate the prophecy of Jesus' coming.

For to us a child is born, to us a son is given, and the government will be on his shoulders. And he will be called Wonderful Counselor, Mighty God, Everlasting Father, Prince of Peace. Isaiah 9:6-7.

Lunchbox Note

December is a very special month. We are going to have lots of fun as a family. Most of all, let's keep thinking about the real meaning of Christmas. We will celebrate Jesus all month!

Second Week of Advent
This is the week we will celebrate Mary and Joseph.

So Joseph also went up from the town of Nazareth in Galilee to Judea, to Bethlehem the town of David, because he belonged to the house and line of David. He went there to register with Mary, who was pledged to be married to him and was expecting a child. Luke 2:4-5

Lunchbox Note

Joseph and Mary were obedient to the awesome job God gave them to do. When you think something is too hard for you, remember how hard it must have been for them. God was faithful to take care of them. He will take care of you, too.

81

Third Week of Advent

This is the week we will celebrate the shepherds.

When the angels had left them and gone into heaven, the shepherds said to one another, "Let's go to Bethlehem and see this thing that has happened, which the Lord has told us about." Luke 2:15

Lunchbox Note

The shepherds couldn't wait to see Jesus.
Let's look forward to celebrating His birth together.

Fourth Week of Advent

This is the week we will celebrate the Kings.

They went on their way, and the star they had seen in the east went ahead of them until it stopped over the place where the child was. When they saw the star they were overjoyed. On coming to the house, they saw the child with his mother Mary, and they bowed down and worshiped him. Then they opened their treasures and presented him with gifts of gold and of incense and of myrrh. Matthew 2: 9–11

Lunchbox Note

(Because of the calendar, some years this note may have to be left on the pillow at night!) The kings, or wise men as they are often called, brought precious gifts to Jesus. What could you give Jesus this year for His birthday?

Christmas Eve

So they hurried off and found Mary and Joseph, and the baby, who was lying in the manger. Luke 2:16

There will be no lunchbox on this day. Just lots of celebrating with family and friends with Jesus as the Honored Guest.

Please note the suggested focus for each week is only that, a suggestion. Many families have come up with their own traditional focuses for each week. Some advent wreath instructions suggest that the theme for each week focus on an aspect of worship. A common plan for this is:

Week One—Hope

Week Two—Love

Week Three—Joy

Week Four—Peace

Optional Center Candle of the Advent Wreath represents Jesus and is to be lighted on Christmas Eve.

A Sweet December

December is a great time to include a special seasonal sweet in the lunchbox. Many of us do a little extra baking for the holidays and can include cookies baked from old family recipes. Others of us do not have big baking traditions and must rely on others to help supply our family sweets. You can start a new lunchbox tradition to be handed down through generations—The Decadent December Lunchbox!

Chocolate dipped cookies. Purchase your child's favorite ready-made cookies. Melt white or dark chocolate candy coating according to package directions. Dip cookies into the chocolate about two thirds of the way up the cookie. Hold for a moment and let excess drip back into the pot. Place on waxed paper to set. Pretzels also work well for this. If you are energetic, you can make your own cookies to dip. But if time is a factor, store bought cookies work well.

Marshmallow snowmen. Attach two large marshmallows together with a pretzel stick. Attach a smaller marshmallow on top for the head. Use a toothpick dipped in food color to make a face and buttons. Use additional pretzels for arms and legs. Be creative and add a hat made from gumdrops or licorice. Colored icing could also be used to decorate your snowman but that increases your preparation time as well as your clean up time!

Christmas snack cakes. Rather than the usual oatmeal pies or peanut butter filled cookies, purchase a box of festive snack cakes for the holidays. They come in white and dark chocolate as well as tree, wreath, and other shapes.

Reindeer candy canes. In just a few minutes a candy cane can be transformed into a smiling Rudolph. With a small red pompom for his nose, two pieces of something black for his eyes, some pipe cleaner antlers, Rudolph the red-nosed candy cane is sure to please your child.

Christmas Trivia

If your child is a trivia buff, he will love having some Christmas trivia included in his lunchbox. Even if trivia is not something he is often interested in, perhaps he will enjoy a few interesting facts of the season. Trivia is great lunchbox fare and often promotes discussions around the lunch table, especially for older children. There are many great books of the season that include information such as the origin of carols and Christmas customs, recipes, favorite stories, and holiday activities. Here's a bit of trivia to get you started. (Trivia taken from **www.coolquiz.com** and from various sites using a Web search for Christmas+trivia.)

Robert May wrote "Rudolph, the Red-Nosed Reindeer" in 1939. Two other names he considered before deciding on Rudolph were Reginald and Rollo.

Lunchbox Note

Can you imagine singing "Reginald, the Red-Nosed Reindeer?"
In early England, a traditional Christmas dinner
was the head of a pig prepared with mustard.

Lunchbox Note

I am glad we eat turkey for Christmas dinner.
I don't think I would like any kind of head!

According to a 1995 survey, seven out of ten British dogs get Christmas gifts from their doting owners.

Lunchbox Note

What shall we give Rufus for Christmas?

Christmas has different meanings in different countries. Christmas Eve in Japan is a good day to eat fried chicken and strawberry shortcake.

Lunchbox Note

I think just about any day is good for eating fried chicken and strawberry shortcake!

The first Christmas card was created in England on December 9, 1842. More than three billion Christmas cards are sent annually in the United States.

Lunchbox Note

Wonder when the first photo card was created? Let's take our picture when you and Dad get home so we can send it to our friends.

During the Christmas season, more than 1.76 billion candy canes will be made.

Lunchbox Note

How many of those billions do you think we eat at our house? We sure do our part!

Theodore Roosevelt, a staunch conservationist, banned Christmas trees in his home, even when he lived in the White House. His children, however, smuggled them into their bedrooms.

Lunchbox Note
Do you think you could smuggle a Christmas tree
into your bedroom? I think I would notice!

It is a British Christmas tradition that a wish made while mixing the Christmas pudding will come true only if the ingredients are stirred in a clockwise direction.

Lunchbox Note

What would you wish while you stir Christmas pudding?

Only nine minutes are spent by the average parents playing with their children on Christmas morning.

Lunchbox Note

I don't want to be average this Christmas.
Let's spend hours together Christmas morning.
Actually, let's start spending some time together
when you get home today.

Ten percent of American households leave milk and cookies for Santa Claus.

Lunchbox Note

What kind of cookies do you think Santa would like this year?

Let's don't forget a carrot for Rudolph.

The classic animal crackers box is designed with a string handle because the animal-shaped cookie treats, introduced in 1902 as a Christmas novelty, were packaged so they could be hung from Christmas trees.

The Twelve Days of Christmas are the twelve days between Christmas Day, December 25, and Epiphany, January 6. Include a special surprise on each of the twelve days.

The poem commonly referred to as "The Night Before Christmas" was originally titled "A Visit from Saint Nicholas." This poem was written by Clement Moore for his children and some guests, one of whom anonymously sent the poem to a New York newspaper for publication.

Dutch children set out shoes to receive gifts any time between mid-November and December 5, St. Nicholas' birthday.

Lunchbox Note

I guess that would be one reason to be thankful for big feet!
Your shoes would hold a lot of candy and presents!

Chapter Four

Love Notes Touch Others

First Note Request

Although lunchbox notes were a staple at our house, it wasn't so everywhere. Tina's request just confirmed their importance.

Ringgggg! Ringgggg!

"Hello."

"Mrs. G, this is Tina. I want to speak to Ginger, please. But first, could I ask you something?"

"Sure, Tina, what is it?"

"Tomorrow do you think you could write me a note? You always put the best notes in Ginger's lunch and nobody ever writes me a note. Would that be too much trouble?"

"Not at all, Tina. I'll be glad to do that. Hold on and I'll get G."

When lunch was packed at our house, the note was just as much a part of the daily lunch as the food. We never felt the lunch was complete unless I had written and carefully placed a note in the bag.

Tina, I wrote, *I hope your day goes well. You are a precious young lady, and you are very special to me. Have a nice day. Love, Mrs. G.*

The following evening the phone rang again.

"Mrs. G?"

"Yes."

"This is Tina. My day went really well today. Thanks for the note. If you ever want to send another one, that would be fine."

"OK, Tina, I'll remember that."

Lunchbox Fact

Notes are only a few words . . . a few simple words that can have a powerful impact on a life.

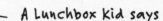

A Lunchbox kid says

Everyone who sat with me at lunch wanted to know what was in my note. When we sat down at the table, they would say, "Hurry up and see what you got today." Not only did those notes make my day, they made the day for all those around me!

—Jaci, age 26

Love Notes Are Passed Along

Dale Hanson Bourke cleaned out her son's lunchbox each evening as part of the preparation for the next day. In her book, *Everyday Miracles,* she recounts the evening she discovered just how special those notes were to her son, Chase. "Each night when I cleaned out Chase's lunchbox, I would find the day's note, with greasy little fingerprints on it. It made me smile to think of him reading each day as he ate his lunch.

One day I opened his lunchbox to find only crumbs and a half-eaten carrot. "Where's your note, Chase?" I asked him.

He looked sheepish. "Sorry, Mom," he said, "I gave it to Jimmy."

"Why?" I asked in confusion.

"Well, I hope you don't mind, Mom, but he never gets a note. So I thought I could share mine with him." Chase looked at me sideways, waiting for my reaction.

He was relieved when I bent down and hugged him. Jimmy's mom was single and worked long hours to support her family. I guessed that spending time to write lunchbox notes was not easy for her. I was proud my son passed his precious note on to Jimmy.

"You're a very special boy," I told him.

"I know," he responded.

All I could do was laugh. I had thought that Chase needed a note each day to remind him of that fact. But not only was he keeping up with his classmates, he was even helping some of them along, too."

Chase experienced the benefit of a note in his lunchbox. He knew how special it made him feel and he wanted to pass that feeling along to his friend. What a sensitive little boy!

When our children begin to pass along the encouragement they receive in their lunchboxes our effort is doubled. But even better, our children have learned how important it is to encourage others.

Guardian Angel

"Mom, can you believe it? You put that little stick-on plaque in my lunch one day when you didn't have time to write a note. I just stuck it to my dashboard last week!"

Kristi came in late from school one day, excited about the end of her day.

"Tell me what happened," I prodded.

"I was sorting uniforms in the band room. I heard that Deanna, Kim, Angela, and two other girls had been in an accident when they left school. As far as anyone knew they were not seriously hurt, only shaken up."

I said a silent prayer for these friends. I remembered that two of them played in Kristi's brass section in the marching band.

About an hour later when they came into the band room, they were still upset but physically unhurt.

"Once Kim quit crying, we sat down." Kristi said.

Kim began telling Kristi how she had been leaning against Kristi's car right before they left the school grounds. Angela came along and they were talking. Kim suddenly remembered the little plaque on Kristi's dashboard and said to her friend, "Angela, listen to this . . . Drive no faster than your guardian angel can fly."

When Deanna came along, the five girls got into Kim's car. They weren't going to be gone long, so they didn't even bother to buckle their seat belts. They took off and headed down the big hill on Dupree Drive.

Kim said to my daughter, "Kristi, just as we started down the hill, I told Deanna and the other girls about the plaque in your car. I told them what it said. About that time, something ran out in front of the car and Deanna slammed on brakes. They locked and we started to skid. We left the road, broke a utility pole in half, and the support wire from the pole kept us from flipping over."

Kristi comforted Kim. "I know you must have been really scared."

"We were." Kim said. "But, Kristi . . . we took your guardian angel with us."

Lunchbox Hint

*Keep a stash of small surprises on hand
for days you don't have time to write a note.
You'll be surprised how God will time even those
surprises to touch lives. I always felt like I was taking the
easy way out by just including a store-bought surprise.
Kristi's lunchbox plaque had a special message.
God intended those girls to see that plaque
and be reminded of His protection.*

Notes for the Whole Class

In her book, *A Letter Is a Gift Forever*, Florence Littauer tells the story of the impact a little boy's lunchbox notes had on his class. Years later, when the teacher was speaking to the little boy's mother, his teacher says, "I will never forget seeing all the children gather round at lunch each day to read those letters. You wrote those letters to Jeremy, but every child received a blessing and wished his mother wrote him notes."

Jeremy's mother had no idea something so simple could make such a difference in a whole grade at Jeremy's school. When she wrote notes of encouragement to Jeremy, she was encouraging the entire fifth-grade class! Jeremy's mom did not feel like she had packed his lunch until she finished the note—it was just part of the daily process.

Ask your child if he is the only one who reads your notes. It's very possible that you are encouraging many more children than just your own.

A Lunchbox Kid says

The notes that I received didn't only offer themselves and their often silly messages to me but to my classmates as well. My classmates would eagerly await lunchtime, too. They often crowded around me to read it over my shoulder as I read it aloud.

—Jaci, age 26

Pam's Scripture Notes

Jennifer's mom wrote notes every day. She worked hard to create fun, entertaining notes for her daughter throughout her lunchbox years. In fact, Jennifer's mom wrote notes to many of Jennifer's friends who ate lunch with Jennifer.

But one day she was moving Jennifer's Bible from one place to another and a collection of love notes fell out and scattered all over the floor. They were not notes from her but from Jennifer's best friend's mother, Pam. Pam also wrote notes to everyone at Jennifer's lunch table. Pam had not been very creative or funny. The notes simply had a verse of Scripture on them. Jennifer had saved each of Pam's notes for years.

Jennifer enjoyed the notes from her mom. They were fun. But she knew over time the notes that would be most dear to her heart would be the Bible verses, love notes from God. Pam had selected those words of wisdom just for Jennifer, and somehow they were always just what she needed for that particular day!

Some of Jennifer's Scripture notes included:

Jeremiah 33:3—*Call to me and I will answer you and tell you great and unsearchable things you do not know.*

94

Psalm 46:1—*God is our refuge and strength, an ever-present help in trouble.*

Psalm 32:8—*I will instruct you and teach you in the way you should go; I will counsel you and watch over you.*

1 Peter 5:7—*Cast all your anxiety on him because he cares for you.*

Psalm 37:4—*Delight yourself in the Lord and he will give you the desires of your heart.*

Ephesians 4:29—*Do not let any unwholesome talk come out of your mouths, but only what is helpful for building others up according to their needs, that it may benefit those who listen.*

1 John 4:19—*We love because he first loved us.*

1 John 2:10—*Whoever loves his brother lives in the light, and there is nothing in him to make him stumble.*

1 John 4:7-8—*Dear friends, let us love one another, for love comes from God. Everyone who loves has been born of God and knows God. Whoever does not love does not know God, because God is love.*

Isaiah 58:9—*Then you will call, and the Lord will answer; you will cry for help, and he will say: Here am I.*

Tuna Can Special

Andrew was in the lunch bunch for years.

Andrew's first note was on the top of a tuna can! He called that evening to say he really appreciated the note, but it was kind of hard to carry the top of a tuna can in your pocket unnoticed. For one thing, it stuck out. For another, it still had a tuna smell. Finally, during sixth period, Andrew decided the tuna can top had to go!

"But," he said, "would you please write me another note some day. Maybe one I could keep?"

Andrew got many notes after that, all on paper. But the day he thought he had finally "arrived" was near the end of the year.

"Wow, Mrs. G," he called to say, "I couldn't believe it. Just a note would have been fine but to have a sandwich *and* a note . . . what a treat!"

It took so little time to dip a toothpick in a bottle of food color and write a few words on top of a sandwich but what a lasting impression.

I recently talked to Andrew. He has graduated from college and is a wonderful architect.

"What kind of lunches do you make these days?" he asked. "I bet they couldn't be as good as the ones with the notes we got when we were in high school, especially the one I got on top of my sandwich!"

A Lunchbox Kid says

These love notes became dear to my friends also, and they were the first thing that we talked about almost every day at lunch. I can't count the number of times one of my girlfriends would ask, "Hey, what did your mom write today?" This was also a perfect opportunity to share my faith to my friends who weren't Christians. Looking back on my high school career, the notes my Mom sent me every-day will always be something dear to my heart!!

—Deb, age 19

Chapter Five

Love Notes Provide a Little Extra Love

Lonely

Margit had just started attending a new school. It was a beautiful school, and she had a nice new teacher and class. But it was all very foreign to her.

Margit's family had moved all the way across the country so her dad could take a new job. Their family was thankful for the job. But it was really hard on Margit and her brother Thomas. They had dreaded the first day in the new school.

Margit had been very quiet all day long. Mrs. Howe, her teacher, had tried to draw her into the class discussion. She had offered for Margit to be her "helper" for the day. But nothing seemed to interest this lonely little girl.

At lunchtime, Margit followed the class into the lunchroom and sat at the end of a table. She looked as if she wanted to get as far away as possible from these strangers who had not yet become friends.

Mrs. Howe watched as Margit opened her lunchbox. She didn't start to eat immediately but began rummaging around as if looking for something very important.

Shortly, Margit's face broke into the first smile of the day. Her little eight-year old hand came up out of the lunchbox and began unfolding a white piece of paper. She read her note and reread her note and then carefully refolded it and placed it back in the lunchbox. With a lingering hint of a smile Margit began to eat her sandwich.

Margit's Lunchbox Note

Have fun at your new school. I am praying for you. You are my special little Margit. Hurry home and we'll unpack more boxes in your new room. Mom

---

A Lunchbox kid says

Once while having the worst day of my life in eighth grade, I literally lost my best friend, got dumped by a boyfriend, made an awful grade on an exam, and had no one to eat lunch with because I just lost my best friend. I opened my lunchbox and saw a crumpled up paper . . . at first I was like, "whatever," but I opened it, and it said "Dear Madison, I love u soo much, and I always will . . . love, mom." Other days I would have been embarrassed by the note but that day I will never forget, because it was just the day I needed to hear that.

—Madison, age 14

Thinking a Class Is Too Hard

I remember well how hard geometry class was. It just didn't make sense to me. And on top of my difficulty in understanding the subject, I felt like the teacher didn't like me.

My teacher was an older woman and thought each of her students should share her aptitude for the subject. She had very little patience for those of us who were more inclined to the arts than to geometry. More than once I was called down and made to feel like the class dunce.

My sister (who did have an aptitude for that sort of thing) spent a lot of time trying to help me understand the workings of triangles and the placement of tangents and whatever else was included in that class. I did the best I could and at least was able to earn a passing grade.

It doesn't take much, however, to make a student feel out of place in a class. Sometimes it is not the teacher. Sometimes other students may make your child feel like the subject is just too hard and impossible to learn. Your love note in her lunchbox can make a tremendous difference. In fact, your notes on the good days are strengthening your child against the bad ones.

Let your child know she can succeed. Let her know that you love her even if things are really tough. Let her know she is special.

Lunchbox Note

I know you have been having a hard time with your spelling (or whatever subject). Spelling was hard for me, too. Keep trying and you will get better and better. Practice makes perfect. (That is an old saying that your great-grandmother used to say to me!) I L-O-V-E Y-O-U!

A Lunchbox kid says

I love getting cards in my lunchbox. My mom has done it many times. If I have a really big test one day and she knows that I'm stressed, it's great to open my lunchbox and see a letter that says, "I love you and am praying for you, love, Mom." It comforts me so much and it makes nervousness go away.

—Teal, age 13

Disappointed

The school years are full of many wonderful accomplishments. There are opportunities to learn in many areas—academics, sports, music, and more. Yet there are also disappointments along the way. You can't win every game, contest, spelling bee, or competition.

Our job as parents (and cheerleaders) is to help our children understand that winning an award or prize does not make them a winner. They are already winners before they ever enter any kind of contest.

When I was a little girl, my dad used to say, "It's not whether you win or lose, it's how you play the game." I never thought about that old sports cliché very deeply until I had children of my own. It is much more than how you play a game. In the game of life, your child is already a winner. But it is up to us to encourage and instruct them as they "play the game" and to help them know that they are winners.

Caz McCaslin, founder and president of Upward Unlimited, defines a winner as someone who is "learning and/or teaching lessons in the game of life." God has put within each of us those characteristics it takes to be a winner. God created winners. As we help our children develop character and self-esteem and plant seeds that will lead them to get to know God, we are in the process of bringing out the winner in each of our children.

What's important in every "game" is that our child put forth his or her best effort. Whether or not an opponent in a game or competition is defeated is not the most important thing.

As our children deal with disappointments, they need most to hear how much they are loved and how special they are. Often, they don't want to talk about the disappointment face to face. But a note slipped into their lunchbox or left on their pillow can make a tremendous difference in how they feel. And, often those are the times seeds of self-esteem are best received.

A Lunchbox Kid says

I received my most memorable "lunchbox note" on a Monday. The Saturday previous to receiving the note, I participated in a band competition for my school, which our band was expected to win because of our size and reputation. However, we did not get many awards and were out-performed by many much smaller bands, so it was an enormous disappointment to those of us who had invested so much time into this activity. I was upset and really felt like a failure, and my mom was aware that it would be hard for me to face colorguard class this particular Monday. So, unbeknownst to me, she slipped a note into my lunch. That morning, as I waited for the bell to ring, I checked to see what my mom had packed for lunch that day, and found a special note. It read:

Dear Amanda,
I just want you to know that I love you, and I am so proud of you. I know you were disappointed with the competition Saturday night, but you

were beautiful and did a great job. Please remember that you are loved and prayed for every single day. Thank you for being such a treasure to my heart.

Love,
Mom

My mom's encouragement meant so much; to know that someone was praying for me when I was feeling like a failure was such an encouragement and really lifted my spirits that Monday. She let me know in such a simple and thoughtful way that I am loved, and that I don't have to win a ton of awards to be loved and treasured. Yes, I was still let down, but I faced the day with a renewed joy because I was reminded of Christ's love by the love my own mother displayed through a note in my lunchbox. I will never forget the impact that this note had on me that day, and in turn, my life.

—Amanda, age 16

Backwards or Out of Sorts

"Aw, Mom," said Keri. "You just don't understand."

"Don't understand? I am listening to what you have told me. Today was just a really bad day. I'm sorry."

"No, Mom, I just couldn't do anything right. Even at recess, I was a klutz. We were playing kickball, and I couldn't even kick the ball when it was sitting still."

Mom looked at Keri, trying to think of something encouraging to say about her day.

"Then," Keri continued, "to top it all off, when we were going back in from recess, I tripped going up the steps. Mrs. Ellis was trying to make me feel better and had asked me to be her helper. I was carrying three kick balls. That wasn't a problem until I tripped. Then the whole class started laughing. The balls rolled back out to the playground, and I had to chase them . . . "

"Oh, Keri," said Mom, "what a day! I'm sure tomorrow will be better."

Mom helped Keri get her stuff out of the car and walked carefully behind her into the house. Mom watched each step Keri took, in case she had to catch something she dropped. She didn't want Keri to know how carefully she was watching her, though. Mom breathed a sigh of relief when Keri finally got in the house. She didn't want home to be a continuation of her playground experience.

When she got inside, Keri turned around. "Mom," she said, "do I have to go to school tomorrow?"

Mom laughed. "Of course, you do. Now get started on your homework!"

Lunchbox Note

Sorry yesterday was such a bad day. Maybe this note will be the only thing backward about today. I think you are just perfect.

I love you. Mom

(This note should be written backwards so your child will have to stand in front of a mirror or hold it up to a sunny window to read it!)

Bullied

We sat around the dinner table, and my usually gregarious seven-year-old didn't say a word. He picked at his food and wouldn't even look at us.

"William," I asked, "what is the matter? You haven't said a word since we sat down at the table. Did something happen at school today?"

William continued to pick at his food.

"William?" His dad didn't usually tolerate rudeness.

"Yes, sir."

I detected a tear forming in the corner of William's eye. I poked his dad with my toe (under the table)—my signal to back off a little.

"School was awful."

"Awful? In what way?" I probed.

Finally the story began to tumble out. There was a bully on the playground at recess. William is not a large child and the kid evidently saw him as an easy target. The bully had pushed William down in front of all of his friends, and then he sat on William's back so he couldn't get up. William was not hurt but terribly embarrassed. Tears streamed down his cheeks as he told us what happened.

We can't protect our children from embarrassing situations, especially once they have entered school. That is why our job as lunchbox scribes is so important. As parents we have to help them be so secure in who they are that incidents like the one that William was involved in at school are only momentary setbacks.

Every word of praise and affirmation counts!

Lunchbox Note

I don't know why some children have such a hard time getting along with others. They probably need someone to love them. I hope your day today is better and you have lots of fun at recess. I will be praying for you.

Discouraged

Another big tear trickled down Ginger's cheek. Oh, Lord, I prayed, Why is every afternoon like this?

Once again I sat in the floor with Ginger, recognizing from her face that what was in her head was not finding the easy way to the paper.

"I can't do it," she said.

"Yes, you can," I replied. "Just try a little harder. Here, start that page over, and I will help you."

"I just can't," she wailed.

Second grade was not Ginger's easiest year. Homework time was always a struggle and became a joint effort with the rest of the family as coaches and cheerleaders! Thanks to an understanding teacher and much determination on Ginger's part, she moved on to third grade.

That was many years ago. Ginger learned how to overcome her difficulties and today proudly displays her college diploma.

But second grade days can be hard. And because of the very basic nature of the lessons, they must be learned well in order to provide a foundation for the rest of the school years.

Lunchbox Note

Hang in there! When something seems hard to understand, don't give up! You can do it. And I support you all the way.

A Lunchbox kid says

Mom started writing notes when I was in grade school but got away from it when I got older. When I got in

high school, I asked her if she would start writing
notes again because I really missed them.

—Jaci, age 26

Tired of School

Sometimes our 180-day school year seems awfully long, especially during the middle of a semester. It seems like Christmas or summer will never get here. But it always does!

When your child gets tired of school, it may be time to start a countdown calendar in the lunchbox.

Lunchbox Note

I know you didn't want to go to school today. But you got up and went anyway. I am proud of you. When you get home, let's do something really fun before you start your homework. Twenty-eight school days to go!

Feeling Not As Smart As Everyone Else

"Mom, I just can't do it. Mrs. Lynch explained that math problem to me three times in class, and I just didn't get it. I am just dumber than everyone else."

Obviously Jared was having trouble in math.

"Oh, yeah, and after that, the class laughed at me because I couldn't get it. I don't think I will go to school tomorrow. Maybe they will forget how dumb I am if I skip a day." Jared's body language just emphasized his dejection.

With several dozen students in almost every class-room, teachers don't always have extra time to spend with individual students. If a student doesn't understand part

106

of a lesson, he is often left on his own to figure out the concept.

Jared was having trouble, and I wasn't a lot of help. The math I did in school was so long ago and not nearly as difficult as my son's. I could understand why he was feeling like he was not as smart as the other kids.

"Jared," I said. "Your older brother is really good at math. When he gets home, I bet he can help you understand how to do this. But until then, I am going to pray for you to catch on very quickly."

Lord, help Jared to understand his math. But more than that help him to understand that it doesn't matter to You or me whether or not he knows math. You love him, and I love him. Help me to let him know how special he is.

Lunchbox Note

*Last night you said you were feeling like everyone was smarter
than you. I don't agree with that. Everybody learns at his
or her own pace and everyone learns differently.
Just figure out which method works best for you.
If you need help, we can work together this afternoon.*

French Class

In our elementary school students begin taking French in the fourth grade. Studying a foreign language at that age is both fun and confusing at times.

Early in Kristi's first year of taking French, frequent "Bonjours!" were heard around our house. As she progressed, new multi-word phrases were included—"Comment allez-vous?" "Ou es ma soeur?" and the like.

It became a new adventure for the entire family. Each of us added a few French words to our rusty foreign vocabularies and tried to find ways to include the lesson of the week in conversation.

Lunchbox Note

You are doing a great job. Listen well in class,
and each day French will be a little easier.
Je t'aime. (I love you.)

Needing an Apology

One morning we were in a hurry. I overslept; the children didn't want to get out of bed; we were out of milk; someone couldn't find his backpack; someone else couldn't find her socks that matched; and the car keys seemed to be hiding. I was short with the kids as I pushed them out the door. The morning was a disaster and the day was off to a terrible start.

Once at school, I hurried everyone out of the car, reminding them to grab their backpacks and lunchboxes, and my "Have a great day, sweetie!" felt less than sincere. I was just anxious to get to work and reach a point of relief at having everyone where they were supposed to go.

By the time we returned home, after piano lessons, soccer practice, and a few other things that demanded our attention, we had to do homework and never really got to discuss the morning. I still felt like I owed the children an apology. So, the next day I made sure I took time to write my apology and slip it into their lunchboxes. A little late is always better than never!

Lunchbox Note

Yesterday I blew it
The morning went askew
And next thing I knew it
My wrath included you!

I want to say I'm sorry
I'll make it up somehow
You're so important to me
Forgive me, please, right now!

Today when school is over
I hope you'll get home fast
Let's spend some time having fun
Before the day is past.

I love you,
Mom

Without Any Friends

Children can be cruel, and one day your child may feel very popular with peers and the next feel like she doesn't have a friend in the world.

Clarissa had one of those days recently. She got off the bus and walked to the door slowly. Looking out the window, her mom could read her body language. Something wasn't right. Usually Clarissa bounced up the sidewalk and bounded through the door with her mouth speaking faster than her mom's ears could listen! Today she wasn't her usual perky little self.

"Welcome home, Rissy," her mom called from the door. "How was your day?"

Clarissa didn't answer immediately. She just shuffled through the door.

"I hate school," she finally said. "Nobody likes me there."

"Aw, Rissy, it can't be that bad," said her mom.

"But it was. When we picked teams at recess, I was the last one. The last one. Nobody wanted me on their team." Her bottom lip quivered.

Her mom reached out and gave her a great big hug. "If I were picking . . . "

Clarissa interrupted, "I know, I know . . . you'd pick me first. But, Mom, you weren't picking. And everybody saw me standing there at the very last. It was awful!"

Clarissa's mom didn't say anything else. She wisely just went into the kitchen and began fixing a very special tea party—sure to cheer up even the most dejected-feeling young lady!

Lunchbox Note

When I was a little girl, Mama used to say, "Nobody loves me; everybody hates me; I think I'll go to the garden and eat worms." It's not so! Did you feel that way yesterday? When you get home, we'll go to the garden. We can eat worms . . . gummi worms! But let's plant flowers, too.

To Talk About Difficult Subjects

As children get older there are some subjects that become difficult to discuss with parents. Conversations may hint at the subject but open, honest communication is avoided. Sometimes a short note will be just the open door needed to spark a discussion.

Don't get specific in the note if your child is accustomed to passing notes around the table at lunch. If your child has been dealing with a difficult friend, situation, teacher, or whatever, he will not want the whole world to know!

Lunchbox Notes

When your child has seemed lonely . . .
You have been extra quiet lately. Want to go for a walk with Bowzer and me after school?

When your child's friend has moved away . . .
Wonder what Jessie is doing at her new school.
Let's write her a long letter this afternoon.

When your child failed a test he felt he was well prepared for . . .
I know you had hoped to do better on your history test.
As far as I am concerned, you are an A+ all the way.

When your child's friends are bad influences . . .
I know it has been hard to stand up to your friends
when they want you to do things that you know are not right.
I am proud of you. You are very courageous.

Chapter Six

Other Types of Love Notes

Scripture Notes

God gave us a whole book full of love notes! So when we can't think of anything to say, we can just borrow one of His. Scripture notes are the very best kind of love notes. They come straight from the heart of our Heavenly Father who loves us more than we can even imagine.

Put one in your child's lunchbox, and include a few sentences of explanation. He will be grateful. And, if your note is passed around the lunch table, seeds will be planted in the hearts of all those who read it.

Lunchbox Notes

- God's Note: *But seek first his kingdom and his righteous-ness, and all these things will be given to you as well.* Matthew 6:33
- Mom's Note: *Before you ask God for anything else, get to know Him by spending time with Him. Try to be like Him. And everything else will fall into place.*

- God's Note: *No one can serve two masters. Either he will hate the one and love the other, or he will be devoted to the*

113

one and despise the other. You cannot serve both God and money. Matthew 6:24

- Mom's Note: Every day you have to make choices. Sometimes those choices are between doing what God wants and what the world or your friends want. Always choose God!

- God's Note: You will keep him (or her) in perfect peace whose mind is stayed on you. Isaiah 26:3 (NKJV)
- Mom's Note: Keep your mind on Jesus. You will be peaceful even when things around you are a mess!

- God's Note: Each one should use whatever gift he (she) has received to serve others, faithfully administering God's grace in its various forms. 1 Peter 4:10
- Mom's Note: Your talents can bless other people. Maybe Mrs. Panell would like you to come over and play the piano for her this afternoon. Her face really lights up when she listens to you play.

- God's Note: See, I have engraved you on the palms of my hands; your walls are ever before me. Isaiah 49:16
- Mom's Note: Look at the palm of your hand. Now close your hand. See what a safe place your palm is. If you have something in the palm of your hand and your hand is closed around it, it will not fall out. You are in God's hand. You will never get out of that safe place!

- God's Note: The Lord is my shepherd, I shall not be in want. Psalm 23:1
- Mom's Note: Just like a shepherd takes care of his sheep, God is taking care of us. He will make sure we have what we need.

- God's Note: *Dear children, let us not love with words or tongue but with actions and in truth. 1 John 3:18*
- Mom's Note: *Sometimes we say we love someone but our actions don't show it. Make sure your actions show what your words say.*

- God's Note: *Look to the Lord and His strength; seek His face always. 1 Chronicles 16:11*
- Mom's Note: *Always trust God. He knows what is best for you and He is bigger than any problem you may have.*

- God's Note: *"Because he loves me," says the Lord . . . "I will protect him, for he acknowledges my name. Psalm 91:14*
- Mom's Note: *Let others know that you love God. God will protect you when you tell other people you belong to him.*

Lunchbox Promises

A promise in your child's lunchbox can provide encouragement that will last through the day. Choose short verses of Scripture that can be remembered even after lunch is finished. Short explanations can help your child remember he can rely on God. (Explanations below are only suggestions. Use words and examples that will mean the most to your child.) Write the promise in a different size or color to emphasize the promise. You may want to choose a different promise each week. Print the verse on enough pieces of paper for a week's worth of notes. That verse will be read every day along with a short love note. By the end of the week, your child will have added one of God's promises to his or her memory bank.

For God's gifts and his call are irrevocable. Romans 11:29

God has given you many gifts. He has given you many talents like singing and playing soccer. He has given us the gifts of love and peace. He has given us gifts of His promises. Those gifts can never be taken away from us.

I can do everything through him who gives me strength. Philippians 4:13

God will give you the strength you need to do whatever you need to do.

For God did not give us a spirit of timidity, but a spirit of power, of love and of self-discipline. 2 Timothy 1:7

Sometimes you feel shy, don't you? I do too. God wants us to be bold—to speak up when we need to say something. So He gives us power and love and self-discipline. When your friends ask you to do something that you know would not please God, speak up. Ask Him to give you courage. When a friend seems to need a kind word, speak up. When your teacher needs encouragement, offer her a helping hand.

Come near to God and he will come near to you. James 4:8

Spend time with God, talk to Him, read His Word. He will be right there with you.

Commit to the Lord whatever you do, and your plans will succeed. Proverbs 16:3

If you try to do something by yourself, it is hard, and lots of times it doesn't even work, does it? When you have a job to do, ask God to help you before you do anything. Ask Him to show you the best way to do it. He will help you get the job done.

My grace is sufficient for you, for my power is made perfect in weakness. 2 Corinthians 12:9

When you think you are too young or too small or too weak to do something, God can give you what you need to do it. God wants us to rely on Him, especially when we think we can't do something.

He will not let your foot slip—he who watches over you will not slumber. Psalm 121:3

God never goes to sleep. So, whatever and whenever we need Him, He is there.

All things are possible with God. Mark 10:27

Don't ever think anything is too hard for God. He can do anything.

Everyone who calls on the name of the Lord will be saved. Romans 10:13

God wants everyone on this earth to know him. But you have to ask Him. He lets us make the choice. But it's very simple, isn't it? Do you have any friends who need to know about God? Maybe you could talk to them after school today. Tell your friends what a difference Jesus makes in your life.

Jesus Christ is the same yesterday and today and forever. Hebrews 13:8

Almost every day has surprises, doesn't it? Your friend finds a new friend, you don't do as well on the math test as you thought, or someone you don't know very well offers you a special snack—there are a lot of things that happen. But Jesus will never change. We can count on Him to be the same and love us more than anyone could today just like He did yesterday and just like He will do tomorrow.

He heals the brokenhearted and binds up their wounds. Psalm 147:3
When you feel sad or lonely or hurt, tell God about it. He can "bandage" all your hurts and make you feel better.

For where two or three come together in my name, there I am with them. Matthew 18:20
When you have something you want to ask God, ask a friend or two (or your Mom or Dad) to pray with you. God will hear your prayers.

And surely I am with you always, to the very end of the age. Matthew 28:20
God will be with us forever.

Lunchbox Lists

Lists are very popular these days. They are popular because they are easy to remember, they are fun, and they put a lot of information in a little space. The idea of a list can be easily applied to the lunchbox. If you don't use lists too often, your child will find them entertaining and fun.

Many books and television shows now use top ten lists. For younger lunchbox kids, I think three to five are enough items on the list. For older kids, you might want to use as many as ten.

Top Three Reasons I Love You
3. You are so cute when you wrinkle your nose.
2. Nobody likes my chocolate chip cookies as much as you do.
1. God picked you out just for me.

Top Five Reasons Our Family Is the Greatest

5. There are four of us and everybody has a partner.
4. We all like to eat at the same restaurant. (You could insert the name of your favorite family restaurant.)
3. Other families don't like syrup on their cornbread.
2. God put us all together.
1. You are in it!

Top Three Reasons I Like to Fix Your Lunch

3. Cafeteria workers don't know your favorite foods.
2. I like to contribute to your school day.
1. It gives me a chance to say, "I love you."

Top Five Reasons You Are My Favorite Lunchbox Kid

5. The freckle on your ear is cute.
4. You sometimes crawl into bed with me on cold mornings.
3. When I am tired, you give me an extra hug.
2. When I run out of something to write about, I just watch you for a while!
1. You're mine!

Top Ten Reasons Why I Love You Best

(from Bowser, the family dog—it would be nice to add a few paw prints to this one.)

10. You don't ignore me.
9. You let me watch cartoons with you.
8. When you brush me, you don't act like my hair has contaminated the world.
7. You feed me almost every day.
6. You don't care if I drip when I drink.
5. When you go outside you take me with you.
4. If I hang around under the table long enough, you will slip me something to eat.

3. You don't fuss about where I dig.

2. You talk to me like I am a real person. Most of the time I understand everything you say.

1. You don't like cats either!

Colorful Love Notes and Lunches

Why not pick a color of the day and let it be the theme not only for the color of your child's note but also for the lunch offerings! This is especially fun for younger children who are just learning their colors and enjoy reinforcement of their lessons. If you can find a napkin that matches the color of the day, include it with lunch. Or write your note on a white napkin in the color of the day. For extra fun, include a toy, sticker, or small surprise (appropriate color, of course).

Red Lunch

Pizza slice with tomato sauce	Radishes
Apple (red delicious, of course!)	Red licorice stick

Orange Lunch

Sandwich with American cheese	Carrots
Cheese curls	Orange slices

Green Lunch

Tuna sandwich with lettuce	Celery
Bell pepper slices	Pickles
Pretzels dipped in hummus	Grapes

Yellow Lunch

Deviled egg sandwich	Banana
Tortilla chips	Lemon cookie

Lunchbox Fact

Aladdin was premature with a few of their
lunchbox kits. One example is the "It's About Time"
lunchbox. This box was based on a television program
that was canceled before the box even hit the store shelves.
This dome-topped box was issued in 1967 . . .
but not many made it out to the public.

Coded Messages

Every child likes to crack a code! So develop a code that
you and your child can use to exchange notes in the
lunchbox and other places.

The simplest code is the letters with corresponding
numbers. A=1, B=2, C=3, and so on. For older children,
you can reverse the numbers. A=26, B=25, C=24, etc. Or
you may want to come up with an entirely different
system. Whatever you use, just make sure to enclose a key
or work it out with your child before lunchtime.

Lunchbox Note

9 12 15 22 5 25 15 21 9
(I love you)

If your child likes word games, simply scramble the
letters of the words in your message. If your child needs
a little help, leave the first letter of each word in place
and scramble the remaining letters.

Lunchbox Note
Yuo aer vyre sepliac!
(You are very special!)

Another version would be to create a note similar to the hangman game. Put the blanks on the note and give your child a list of the missing letters. He can make the words by supplying the missing letters.

Lunchbox Note

_ _ _ _ _ _ _ _ _ _ _ _ _ ! _ _ _ _ _ _ _ _.

VEAH   A   TRAEG   YAD   I   VEOL   UOY

(Have a great day! I love you!)

Coupons

Some days it is nice to receive something other than a note. On those days, a coupon for time spent with you would be most welcome. Often the problem with coupons is that they are forgotten and never used. But as long as you remember it, you can help your child remember. Coupons could be for anything, but my lunchbox kid always liked a gift of time best.

You can make a classy coupon by downloading some clip art of a coupon and inserting your information. Once you have the coupon form, you can easily change what the coupon is good for.

Suggested Lunchbox Coupons:

This coupon entitles _(Child's Name)_ to one trip to get ice cream on the way home from school.

This coupon entitles _(Child's Name)_ to have a story read tonight after homework is finished.

This coupon entitles _(Child's Name)_ to go for a long walk before doing homework. This coupon may only be used once.

This coupon entitles _(Child's Name)_ to leave one thing on the dinner plate that is not on the list of favorite foods, vegetables included.

This coupon entitles _(Child's Name)_ to one game of _(Child's favorite game)_ before beginning homework.

This coupon entitles _(Child's Name)_ to ask Mom or Dad to feed _(Child's dog or cat)_ one time before the end of the year.

This coupon entitles _(Child's Name)_ to go fishing with Dad anytime he can get off work.

This coupon entitles _(Child's Name)_ to ask Mom to finish washing dishes one night this month.

Puzzle Creations

The amount of time your child has for lunch varies from year to year or school to school. When you hear stories of food fights, being in trouble for talking too loudly, dissatisfaction with the company at the table, you know there is extra time at lunch.

Next time you go to the store, grab a bag of alphabet pasta. Spell out the message the night before on the kitchen cabinet. Then enclose a note for your child with only the first letters of the words. If it is a long message, include blanks for each letter in each word. Then put the pasta along with the note in a plastic zipper bag so none of the letters will get lost.

When your child gets to lunch, she will have a word puzzle to occupy her time and entertain her lunch bunch!

Alphabet cereal will also work. But if there is something heavy in the lunchbox and it rolls over on the cereal, there is the possibility of the "puzzle" being smashed to bits!

A Lunchbox kid says

My grandfather had a business making notepaper cubes for businesses. So we always had paper around the house. Mom would take one of those square pieces of paper and begin on the outside edge. She would write around and around and end in the middle. It was so much fun reading those notes!

—Jaci, age 26

Quick Enclosures

When your morning is rushed and there's not even time to scribble an "I love you," there are still options for perking up the lunch. Keep a stash on hand of things that can be stuck in the lunchbox with little effort.

Suggestions of quick add-ins:

Preprinted Cards—Some stationery stores have displays of small notes of encouragement suitable for inclusion in lunchboxes. There are also several Web sites that offer note cards and paper created especially for lunchbox notes.

Joke Cards—Often discount or dollar stores will carry decks of cards that are different from regular playing cards. Joke cards usually have a joke or riddle on one side and the answer on the other. These make entertaining enclosures for the entire lunch bunch.

Optical Illusion Cards—One toy store I visited had a deck of optical illusion cards. These worked great in the lunchbox. My son's lunch bunch had quite a discussion over the correct interpretation of the illusion. Like the joke cards, these had the illusion on one side and usually included an instruction. Then the flip side told the correct perception.

Magic Tricks—One year I found small, shrink-packed magic tricks. These were simple, required no additional materials to perform, and could be done by even young children. These always needed a word of caution: Be sure to put the trick back in the lunchbox when lunch was over!

Kid's Meal Leftovers—Sometimes when we stopped for fast food, even the older kids ordered kid's meals. When cleaning out the car, I would find the hamburger wrapper, the fry bag, and the long-forgotten toy. I put those in a drawer and included them in lunches when I needed a quick surprise.

Cereal Prizes—Breakfast never included the luxury of digging out and playing with the toy in the bottom of the cereal box, so I retrieved it and put it in the "surprise drawer!" Especially when the kids got older (high school), they really got a kick out of the little toys and puzzles. (Actually, they probably enjoyed them more then than when they were younger! I found them hooked to backpacks, riding around on dashboards, etc.!)

Decorative Papers

Many school supply stores have a good inventory of notepads in colorful, cut-out shapes. They are easy, bright additions to the lunchbox. You can incorporate the shape into the note if you like. For example, use a pad in the shape of an apple to say "You are the apple of my eye!"

Carter, age five, had a note from his dad. "I can't wait to put the lights on the Christmas tree with you tonight." A Christmas tree pad would make a nice background for that note.

- A heart could say "I love you" even without words!
- A star would be a great way to say "You are a winner!"
- A flower could say "Hurray, it's spring!"

Printable notes can be found online. You can print them on your home computer. (See appendix for suggested sites.)

Lunchbox Note

(Paper in the shape of a house.)
Can't wait until you get home. I love you!

A Lunchbox Kid says

My mom used a piece of paper in the shape of grapes. It said, "Have a grape, great day!"

—Andrew, age 5

Cut-Out Messages

Notes don't necessarily have to be in words. A carefully prepared and customized sandwich says "I love you" and "I think you are special." Here are some suggestions for unique holiday lunchbox sandwiches.

Cut-out sandwiches are best created from peanut butter and jelly or pimento cheese sandwiches or some other type of filling that will help hold the bread together. Pull out your cookie cutters or grab a knife and cut out freehand.

Valentine's Day—A heart
September—A football
March—A Shamrock
October—A pumpkin
April—An Easter egg
November—A leaf
May—A flower
December—A Christmas tree

For other occasions:
• When young children are studying shapes, send their sandwiches cut in circles, rectangles, or triangles.
• When young children are studying colors, cut the sandwich into fourths and put a colored dot in the middle of each section with a toothpick dipped in food color.
• For birthdays, cut the sandwich into pieces the shape of the number of the birthday.
• For days when you want something a little extra special, cut the sandwich into the shape of the first letter of the child's name.
• To applaud your student for an accomplishment, cut the sandwich into the shape of a star.

Sticker Notes

Stickers can add pizzazz to your lunchbox notes. When you see inexpensive stickers or receive them free in the

127

mail, in cereal boxes, or at church, save them in the surprise drawer until needed.

Smiley faces—One of my favorites because when we see a little smiley face, we tend to smile back! A smiley sticker could be placed on the napkin with a note, "You make me smile!" or "When I think of you, I smile!"

Star—Use several with a note: "I thank my lucky stars that you are my son/daughter!" Or just a short "You are a star in my book!" will do.

Butterfly—"You are one of God's incredible creations!"

Heart—"You may be at school, but you are never away from my heart!"

A Number One—"You are number one to me!"

Figure stickers could be placed on the inside of the lunchbox lid and a conversation "bubble" added. Then you could put your message inside the bubble to give your note of the day a little different look. Stickers that work well for this are gingerbread men, angels, boys, girls, sports figures, dancers, and animals.

A Lunchbox kid says

My favorite sticker has always been the rose on the bottom of my television. Mom put it there when she went out of town when I was in high school. After I got married, that television was in my bedroom. When I saw the rose, I was reminded how much my family loves me.

—Kristi, age 27

Fruit Notes

Have lunches become a little boring? Maybe a fruit note will save the day.

Apple—Include a note with the apple that says, "You are the apple of my eye."

Banana—A note can be written directly on the banana peel. A gel pen works best. Don't bear down too hard or you will pierce the skin.

Orange—Cut the orange in slices for ease of handling. Include a note that says, "Orange you glad we have each other?"

Grapes—A typical note could be "Have a grape day!"

Pear—"Why don't we pair up when you get home and have some fun?"

Candy Notes

Sometimes it is fun to put a little extra surprise in the lunchbox. Here are a few suggestions.

A stick of gum

Lunchbox Note

I'll stick with you forever!

A Snicker candy bar

Lunchbox Note

I never snicker when I think of you.

A chocolate "kiss"

Lunchbox Note

Here's a kiss from Mom/Dad

A chocolate "hug"

Lunchbox Note

Hope this hug will get you through the day!

Lifesaver

Lunchbox Note

You sure were a lifesaver when you
helped me finish the dishes last night.

Million Dollar Bar

Lunchbox Note

You are one in a million!

Three Musketeers bar

Lunchbox Note

You and Daniel and Pete are just like the "three musketeers!"

Twix Bar

Lunchbox Note

Just twix you and me, I think you are very special.

Dum-Dum Sucker

Lunchbox Note

You're no dum-dum. Good luck on your test today!

Nestle Crunch

Lunchbox Note

Remember, I am always here if you get in a crunch!

Napkin Notes

When you finish packing lunch and begin to look around for a piece of paper to write on, look no further than the lunchbox! Napkins make great notepaper, and they are sure to be seen (unless your child forgets to wipe his or her mouth after eating!)

For a sure to-be-remembered note, cut the napkin into a special shape. It may be something that has meaning to your child. Or cut it into the shape of the star when he or she has done something outstanding.

Write directly on the napkin. It only takes a few words to bring a smile to your child's face.

Use a sticker. It could be a sports sticker on game day. Or it could be a sticker that reminds him of a member of

131

the family. Perhaps a dog sticker that depicts the breed of the family pet.

If you are adept with the scissors, cut paper dolls from the napkin for your child. You may want to include an extra napkin if you do this because your child will not want to mess up the cut out napkin!

For a birthday or other special occasion, hide confetti inside the napkin. When your child picks up his napkin, he will enjoy the unexpected celebration. Some stores carry message confetti in the card section that says "Happy Birthday." Or you can make your own using colored paper and a hole punch.

Lunchbox Note

No matter what shape you feel like you are in,
I think you are tip top. I love you!

Note Kabobs

Have you given a dinner party recently and wonder what to do with the left over kabob skewers? Why not turn them into a note kabob for the lunchbox?

Fruit Kabob—Write a note and fold carefully. You can write directly on parchment or waxed paper with a permanent pen or write on regular paper and fold inside a layer of waxed paper. Insert skewer into note. Alternate different pieces of fruit (could also be left from the dinner party). Use grapes, melons, pineapple, or whatever is your child's favorite. If you choose apples, be sure to dip them in lemon or pineapple juice so they will not turn brown.

Meat and Cheese Kabob—Write note and secure to the skewer the same way as for fruit kabobs. Alternate pieces of meat and chunks of cheese on the skewer. The meat could include sandwich meat folded accordion style or leftover chicken. Chunks of hamburger also work, but I don't find hamburger as appetizing when it is cold!

Veggie Kabob—Same idea as above but use carrot slices, celery chunks, cherry tomatoes, broccoli florets, and slices of squash.

Dessert Kabob—Use brownie hunks, cookie pieces, and anything else that would go together to satisfy the sweet tooth!

Whatever kabob you choose, remember to break the point of the skewer off once you have the kabob assembled. This will avoid any potential problems with the sharp point.

Sandwich Notes

"Ginger, something is wrong with your sandwich. Look at that green on it!" Jimmy was always quick to point out when something was not quite right.

"What are you talking about?" Ginger asked as she took another bite.

"It has green on it. Yuk!"

Ginger turned her sandwich around to show the lunch bunch. I had gotten a little carried away this morning with Ginger's lunchbox note. Instead of finding a piece of paper and pencil, I had just grabbed a toothpick and bottle of food coloring. The bright colors showed up really well on the white bread.

I dipped the toothpick into the food coloring and wrote "I love you" on the outside of the sandwich. The first and last few letters were written in green and the "love" was written in red. It did make a very colorful sandwich.

Once I learned the technique of sandwich writing, I tried other designs! I did find, however, that my sandwich notes had to be pretty short. There's not much room on a sandwich and there's not much control over a toothpick!

Hints for sandwich notes:
• A toothpick will not hold much color so you will have to dip it a number of times.
• White bread works best.
• Keep your note brief—a smiley face, I love you, C ya, or some personal logo.
• Let dry a few seconds before putting in the sandwich bag. Most of it will soak into the bread but you don't want it all over the bag!

A Lunchbox kid says

My personal favorite notes were the ones written directly on my sandwich. Those always attracted a lot of attention with the lunch bunch!

—Ginger, age 24

Pizza Puzzle

"Mom, oh, Mom!" Jeff burst through the back door. "How did you do that?"

"Do what?" I asked.

"The kids at my table couldn't believe I had a puzzle made out of a pizza for lunch. That was so cool."

Leftover pizza was always a favorite lunch (or breakfast) at our house. I personally don't think it is very tasty cold, but all those under the age of fifteen love it!

When packing Jeff's lunch that morning, I had taken the pizza cutter and cut his slice of pizza into four irregular shaped pieces. Then I included a note that challenged him to put his pizza back into the shape of a slice before eating. I provided an extra napkin for this activity.

Large sandwiches could also be cut in the shape of a puzzle as could brownies and snack bars. Just be sure to use something that will not crumble into unrecognizable shapes!

Lunchbox Hint

Find creative ways of lunchbox "presentation." Providing the pizza puzzle gave Jeff an opportunity to eat his "appetizer" of carrot sticks while he put his puzzle together. When he was ready to eat the pizza, it was already carved into manageable-sized pieces. And, he was the envy of the lunch bunch with his pizza puzzle!

Smiley Faces

Do your children have special interests? Or a special collection?

My children each have their "thing."

Kristi is an avid Garfield collector. Her room at one time held over a thousand pieces of Garfield memorabilia. Garfield sticky notes often provided the base for her lunchbox notes.

Jeff is a drummer and plays several other instruments. It is easy to find musical toys and note paper to include in his lunch.

Ginger loves smiley faces. Anytime we see a smiley face we think of her or we look at one another and say "Ginger would like that!" Her collection includes pillows, shams, clocks, watches, stationery, notebooks, posters, T-shirts, and lots more.

Any time I go into a store and see anything with a smiley face on it, I usually spend some time there. I went into a discount store one day and saw an entire rack of smiley face stickers, I knew I had to have them. I wasn't sure how I would use so many, but I purchased them anyway, sure that they would be put to good use.

One day I was strapped for time assembling lunches for the next day. I pulled out the stickers and stuck one on the outside of the sandwich bag, one on the napkin and one on the wrapper of her dessert snack cake.

When Ginger arrived home that day, she said, "I sure had a smiley lunch!"

I said, "Did you have a smiley day?"

With a grin she replied, "Of course!"

Lunchbox Hint

Collect stickers that will be especially meaningful to your child and keep them on hand for days when you don't have time to write a note. If your child is a sports enthusiast, find stickers from the sport she enjoys. If she is a pet lover, find stickers of her favorite animal.

Logos

Most businesses have a distinct logo, a pictorial symbol of what they do or a way of writing their initials that is distinct. When people see a certain checkmark, they immediately think of a particular brand of tennis shoes. When they see two yellow arches, they think of a popular fast-food chain.

When my children see a rose, they think of me. Several years ago Rose came to visit our house (see story in chapter one about Rose's development). Very quickly, Rose not only established her identity but also a logo to go along with it. When my children see a rose of any sort, they think of me. But when they see my crude, hand-drawn version of a rose, they know I have been there! Often in their lunches all that is necessary is a rose sticker on their napkin or sandwich bag.

If you take a walk around our house, you will find rose stickers. Not because I have a thing about decorating with stickers. I have strategically placed them to say "I love you" to someone, probably when I was going to be away for a day or so.

At this moment we could visit my son's closet where a rose is stuck to the outside ledge of his eye-level shelf. Or my daughter's bathroom where a rose sticker still resides, faded from years of steam and cleaning the mirror. Look inside my husband's medicine cabinet where his rose is the first thing that greets you!

If you visited my married daughter's bedroom, you would see stuck to the base of her television, you guessed it, a rose!

Just last night I received a new package of rose stickers from one of my children. "Thought you might need these!" she said.

Once you develop a logo, buy stickers, little toys, plastic figures, or anything else that even remotely resembles your logo.

Having a logo that you and your children use freely gives you opportunity to share your story with others as well. "Why is there a rose sticker there?" I have been asked many times. Then I can share the story of how Rose has enhanced my relationships with all my children.

When my son became old enough to sit with a friend in church, I found a seat several rows behind the two boys. At one point they were so absorbed in conversation they could not possibly be getting anything out of the service. I wrote a note, signed it with Rose's logo and passed it three rows forward. They read it, turned around, smiled at me, and were quiet the rest of the service. Had Mom signed the note, I don't think they would have smiled at the reminder to stop talking!

Logos will carry over into all parts of your family life. Like nicknames, some will stick longer than others. But finding creative ways to leave your mark will not be soon forgotten.

A Lunchbox kid says

The notes I remember most are the ones with a hand-drawn eye, a heart, and a big U. That was followed by a rose. I loved seeing that rose. No one else knew what it meant but me!

—Jeff, age 19

Love Songs

When I was a new mother, my favorite time of the day was feeding time. My daughter and I nestled down in the big, green recliner and got all comfy. Then we spent the next fifteen minutes or so in our own little world.

While she nursed, I sang, and we feasted our eyes on one another as if no one else existed in the world. It was a very special time. Though she could not understand the words I was singing, she no doubt heard and felt the love in my voice.

I remember the joy and pleasure I felt as I rocked that precious baby girl and each of her siblings that followed. There was definite delight involved! There were many times that I believe my infant hummed along, even though she could not speak words yet.

As the children got older I continued to sing "over them."

We had several special songs they quickly learned. I guess their favorites were the ones that we made up to other tunes and inserted their names.

No matter how old your child is, it is not too late to "sing" over him. I don't think it necessarily has to be musical singing. The delight in your voice can be melodious to your child as you praise and thank God for the blessing of being a mom or dad.

The Lord your God is with you, he is mighty to save. He will take great delight in you, he will quiet you with his love, he will rejoice over you with singing. Zephaniah 3:17

Nicknames

At our house everyone has a nickname. It may be as simple as "Bud" or "Daddio" or as complex as "Kickalick" or "Peanuttio." Perhaps your nickname for your child will spark your creativity in the lunchbox.

Peanuttio originally came from the nickname of Peanut. For some reason we like the ring of the "io" on the end. For a while peanuts were her trademark. We included peanuts in everything. We gave her bags of peanuts. We drew pictures of peanuts dressed for special days.

Kickalick wasn't as easy to find something to relate

to. But she played the French horn and that became her symbol for a while.

These are fun things that can be included in the lunchbox to remind your children that they are special to you. Many people call them by their given names but the special nicknames are reserved for the family. Only you know the love behind the name!

Take advantage of your child's nickname when packing the lunchbox. Always include something that says to them, "You are special, and I'm glad you are mine!" It may be a note or it could be a bag of peanuts!

Lunchbox Note

God knew I would love a "Peanut."
You are a precious gift from Him.

Lunchbox "Business Cards"

Now that so many moms and dads have computers, it is very simple to make cards to include in your child's lunch. You can do it quickly and easily, and you can make enough cards for several weeks at a time. Then, on busy mornings, you can grab a ready-made note for the lunchbox.

Purchase plain, printable business cards at an office supply or discount store. Usually there are ten on a sheet and have several sheets in a package. Once you print on the cards, they can easily be separated at the perforations.

Here are some suggestions for messages to put on your card.

• I'm thinking of you. Have a great day!

• A verse of Scripture. If your child has a specific verse for the year, include that one. If not, some great verses to include are:

—*If any of you lacks wisdom, he should ask God, who gives generously to all without finding fault, and it will be given to him.* James 1:5

—*But those who hope in the Lord will renew their strength. They will soar on wings like eagles; they will run and not grow weary, they will walk and not be faint.* Isaiah 40:31

—*Be strong and courageous. Do not be terrified; do not be discouraged, for the Lord your God will be with you wherever you go.* Joshua 1:9

—*I thank my God every time I remember you.* Philippians 1:3

—*Let your light shine before men, that they may see your good deeds and praise your Father in heaven.* Matthew 5:16

—*For he (God) will command his angels concerning you to guard you in all your ways.* Psalm 91:11

—*I can do everything through him who gives me strength.* Philippians 4:13

• I'll be praying for you today. Have a good one.

• See you when school is over. I'll be praying for you.

• You studied so hard last night. I am really proud of you.

• I am blessed to have you as my daughter/son.

• Good luck on your test! I'll be praying for you.

You may even surprise your student with a personal business card. Include one of your student's special interests and list the occupation as "student" or "world's greatest kid." You may find that they think it is cool to have a business card of their own that they can share with friends.

Newsletters

Some days require a little extra time and creativity. One of the hits at our house has been my newsletters. Here's my step-by-step formula for a newsletter that will, for sure, be passed around the table.

• Make a list of three or four newsworthy family events of the last week—sports events, haircuts, raking the yard, cutting the grass, baking cookies, a birthday, giving the dog a bath . . . that sort of thing. This is not a quest for national news but a time to spotlight small family events in a fun way.

• Find a computer program, such as Microsoft Publisher, that has a newsletter template already prepared for you. Then you can just insert your own information.

• Give the newsletter a catchy title. It could include the family name or the name or nickname of your hometown.

• Report the "news," making sure the child's name appears frequently in every article.

• One-page newsletters are best. That is probably all there is time to read! And you can save some news for a later issue!

Gibberish

One of the talents I developed in my teen years was that of speaking gibberish. I don't know who invented gibberish but it could have been the same person who came up with Pig Latin.

Gibberish and Pig Latin are similar. Both take the word you are trying to say and combine it with other sounds to form the word in that language.

When I finally caught on to the method, I became fluent in gibberish, and the language was a secret way for me and my friends to communicate. You had to train your ear to pick out the words that were hidden in the conglomeration of sounds.

To speak gibberish, take the word you want to say and divide it into syllables. Speak the first consonant sound of the first syllable, add *th*, then say the rest of the syllable with a *g* in front of it. So, if you wanted to say Mom, it would become *M-th-gom*.

On one particular occasion, I had a gathering of all my nieces and nephews. They were so glad to see each other that they didn't want to quiet down, even for the blessing. Finally, I began to pray . . . in gibberish. They stopped talking, started listening, and with the final *A-th-gah m-th-gen*, broke into gales of laughter!

"What were you saying, Aunt Linda?" They all wanted to know what language I was speaking, and what I had said.

So you might want to try writing your note in another language, maybe even a secret language that only you and your child understand!

Lunchbox Note

Y-th-gou a-th-gare a-th-guh c-th-gool k-th-gid.
Uh-th-gI l-th-gove y-th-gou. (*You are a cool kid. I love you.*)
You may need to practice a little before you start writing in gibberish.

Poetry Notes

Sometimes it just doesn't seem adequate to scribble a few words on a napkin or a little piece of paper. Some days are just poetry days!

Even if you are not super creative, you can borrow a few lines and insert your own special words.

Here are a few examples:

Roses are red,
Flags have some blue,
Hurry on home,
It's lonesome without you!

I know you had a test,
And I'm praying just for you.
When you get home, you can rest
And have a big snack, too.

Have a good day,
As you work and play.
Learn a whole bunch.
And enjoy your lunch!

Though I can't speak,
I still can write.
Have a great day.
See you tonight!

Hi to the lunch bunch.
Have fun as you all munch!

See you soon; Have a great day!
Hurry home, study then play.
You're so special; you're one of a kind!
I'm always so proud to say that you're mine!

Notes from the Family Pets

Jennifer often receives notes from Butch, the family dog.
Any time Jennifer begins to open a note and it feels like it

144

has gravel in it, the sender is probably Butch. Jennifer knows that Butch probably put some of his dog biscuit in the note for her!

Butch occasionally helps Jennifer's mom with the daily note. Once the note is written, Jennifer's Mom puts the note along with a dog biscuit in Butch's favorite chair. In an effort to quickly clear the chair, Butch slobbers all over the note, walks all over it and sometimes even tears it into little pieces. He doesn't care for the dog biscuits so the crumbs and pieces of the biscuit become part of his signature!

Note from Butch

Thanks for brushing me last night. I am really shiny!
Woof, woof! Can't wait for you to get home. Arf, arf!
(Sign by drawing a paw or letting
Butch step on the note with a muddy paw.)

Fluff is another occasional note writer. As the family feline, she is queen of the house. She sleeps with Amy and is very attached to her. Often Fluff sulks from the time Amy leaves for school until she gets home. So in order to ease her loneliness, Mom helps Fluff write a lunchbox note!

Note from Fluff

Meow! Meow! I am so lonesome. Hurry up and
get home from school. There is no one here with me,
and I want a warm leg to rub up against!
That always makes me purr!

145

Notes from Working Moms and Dads

Perhaps you pick up the kids at school and return home from work just in time to eat a take-out supper, start a load of clothes, help with homework, and get everyone to bed. Then you fall into the bed exhausted, never thinking about lunch, much less writing a love note to go in it. How can you communicate with your child while you are apart those long hours?

Look for small surprises at the grocery store. Even though your child does not take lunch to school, special "messages" can be tucked into the backpack, notebook, or coat pocket. Or leave one in the refrigerator taped to the after-school juice box or snack. Most grocery stores have a good supply of stickers, cards, small toys, and the like that make good surprises. A small travel pack of your child's favorite cookies would also be welcome. Knowing that you selected something just for him will make your child feel special.

Bookstores and gift shops have packs of cards to encourage others. I have bought packs that say: "I'm thinking of you;" "You are special;" "I love you;" and many other messages to make someone's day. Once I found a box of cards geared specifically to school children. They contained messages like "Way to go," "Have a nice day," "Good luck on your test," and the like. That was very helpful when I needed a note and had little time.

Do you have access at work to email? When my son took a basic computer class, one of the things they covered was the internet and how to use it. They included email in the lesson. I knew his class met right after lunch. One day I was sitting at my computer and I received an instant message from him. "Just thought I'd say hi," it read. From then on, whenever I could, I was at the computer during that hour. We began to instant message every day we could. It was never long, just a few sentences, but a wonderful means to keep in touch.

Likewise, I also use the regular email system along with the instant messenger to send notes to my children. Sometimes they can read them at school during computer class, sometimes they get them when they get home. Rarely am I present when they are read. But always it serves as a connecting point.

That's really what all this is about—connecting with your child. Whether it is through a love note in his or her lunchbox, an email, a sticker on the bathroom mirror, or a smile across the room, your connection with your child needs to be continually strengthened. And the little things are just as important as the big ones. The building blocks to the foundation of his or her character and self-esteem do not come as boulders. They are small stones placed securely on one another over time. As each one is carefully positioned, your child's character and self-esteem are elevated.

Working moms and dads have just as much opportunity to contribute to that foundation as stay-at-home moms and dads. Sometimes you just have to work a little smarter and be a little more creative with the time you have!

Special Notes

Our annual youth missions trip always ends with what our Youth Minister calls an Affirmation Service. Each work group sits together in the chapel. When the service begins, each individual has a turn when all the other group members come by and speak words of encouragement and affirmation to the person.

One year I was sitting at the front of the church and could observe several groups closely. The front group on the left side of the church immediately caught my attention.

Mark had been a group member of this trip for several years. He sat on the front row for his "turn." One by one the rest of his work group came up behind him, put their hands on his shoulders, leaned over and handed him a note.

Solemnly and carefully, Mark unfolded each note. These were not little scraps of paper. They were full notebook paper sheets. Mark read each word, often going back and forth between a smile and an occasional tear.

You see, Mark was deaf and his group had cared enough to take the time to write notes so that Mark would not miss out on the affirmation process. A few minutes spent crafting a note had a tremendous and maybe even lifetime effect on this young man.

Sample note of affirmation

Mark, you have made a difference in our group.
It would not have been the same without you.
All the children have seen Christ's love in you.
You were so kind and thoughtful to them.
Thanks for being a very important part of our group.

Chapter Seven

Beyond the Lunchbox

Locker Love Letters

Even preschoolers have lockers. Lockers for coats, take home papers, lunchboxes, and stuff. Maybe your child doesn't take lunch every day and you are trying to figure out how to provide a word of encouragement without the lunchbox. Perhaps the locker will give you the opportunity.

Preschool lockers are often open and without doors. They are located in the classroom or hall. When the lockers are in the hall, you can easily slip a note in the cubby or tape a note to the edge of the locker. Just remember that your preschooler will need either very simple words or a pictorial note! A sticker that will be recognized as being from you will also work.

Elementary school lockers are almost always in the halls and have doors. Whether or not your child has a locked locker is probably your choice. Notes can still be taped to the outside of the locker or slipped through the ventilation slits on the door. If you have the opportunity to get inside the locker, tape a timeless note of encouragement that can be seen every time the locker is opened.

Older children almost always have locks on their lockers so you have to be a little more creative! (In fact, some schools require locks on the lockers.) You may have to write your note a day or two ahead of when you want it delivered. Then ask for the help of a close friend. Ask him to slip the note through the slots when your child is not around. If you know the combination of the lock, you could deliver it yourself after school one day. One word of info: I found that my high school children did not go to their lockers very often. In fact, I don't think my son ever used his locker. Because of the location of his classes vs. the location of his locker, it was more convenient to carry most of his books with him and keep the few he would only need occasionally in his car. Therefore, notes in his locker were never found!

Locker Note

If you have access to the inside of the locker, tape a small mirror inside with the note—"You are looking at the most outstanding (cutest, most special, most unique, or any combination of words you might choose) student at this school."

A Lunchbox Kid says

While cleaning my locker out one day, I grabbed all the trash to throw it away. I walked to the trash can and canned all my papers but one missed the trash can. I went to get it to throw it away and noticed the writing was not my style. Curious, I opened it and began reading one of the most important things anyone has ever said to me. They commented on how I had impacted their life, on how I lived a Christian lifestyle, and how I always spoke to people in the hallways even if we weren't friends. To this day I still don't know who wrote it, but I will never forget that people notice my actions and someone is watching me everyday, so I need to set an example.

—Madison, age 14

College Notes

Just because the children leave home and go to college, doesn't mean your note-writing days are over! Actually, they are more important than ever.

My daughter stopped by her college mailbox every day after lunch. The path back to her dorm from the cafeteria went right by the campus post office. When I learned that, I made a concentrated effort to make sure there was something in the mailbox most days.

One mother I know actually mails something every day to her college daughter. When my children went off to college, I felt the same need until one particular conversation with our college son about campus life. He was catching me up on how things were going, etc. Then he said, "Mom, I sure had a lot of mail when I checked my box the other day."

"A lot of mail?" I asked. "I only write a couple of times a week."

"I know," Jeff said with a grin, "but I only check my mail box about once a month. I do everything online now."

Once a month. That was good info to have. I had been working very hard to make sure that Jeff received several pieces of mail each week. What was happening was that he was getting a bundle every now and then. It was at that point I decided maybe there were other things I could do to maintain a presence in the college life of my son.

Continue to Use the US Mail Service

I didn't stop writing just because Jeff didn't check his box often. But I adjusted my frequency of writing to his frequency of checking! Try to include a surprise in each letter so he will look forward to going to the mail box. These surprises can be simple—a newspaper clipping of a hometown event, a sticker, a notepad you have picked up in the shape of something he likes.

Also remember to send a surprise box every now and then. It doesn't have to be big or elaborate. It can include things like snacks, noodles, candy, a new type of pen, or a program from a missed event. Homemade goodies are always welcome.

College care packages, full of reminders of home, are fun for students to receive. Favorite snacks, noodles, soups, popcorn, and other microwavable foods that save them from eating in the cafeteria are popular. Candy canes at Christmas, candy corn in the fall, and Easter marshmallow chicks mail well. My recent college graduate reminded me that any food is welcome to a college student but homemade is always best!

Recognize Special Occasions

Special occasions are different in the college setting and are perfect opportunities to express your love to your child.

Fall Break—Fall break comes and a ray of hope comes into a mother's heart that her college child will come home and want to spend the entire long weekend with her, catching up on all the news. The reality is that your child is so excited to be out of school for a few days that a plan is probably already in place to get away with friends.

Open your home to your student and several friends, offering to be home base for some neat day trips. And, if you are not taken up on your offer, plan to provide a meal on one end of the trip or the other. Be sure to bake his favorite cookies for the trip. You may as well send along the recipe, too, as someone will surely want to duplicate your culinary talent!

Parents Weekend—Tailgating is likely a part of this weekend. Be sure to cook all the favorite foods and take plenty for friends. For the students, the most fun part of the picnic is going from tailgate to tailgate!

Exam Time—This has become a wonderful time for us to say "I love you" and "I'm thinking about you" to our students. In fact, exam popcorn has become a much looked-for and appreciated tradition in our family.

When we had our first college student, my husband wanted her to know he was praying for her during this stressful time. He ordered a big tin of popcorn, buttered, cheese, and caramel, and had it sent to her college address. The big package was a great surprise and the "brain food" was most welcome!

One of our daughters commented that since she is not a neat freak, her box often sat in the middle of the floor for days. When people came in her dorm room to socialize they had to walk around the box. There was never a card enclosed with the popcorn; the message was always written on the top of the box. So as people stepped over the box, they usually read the message. Our daughter said everyone who read it thought it was a really neat thing for her to receive "exam popcorn."

Recently exam time came around again. Now one daughter is finishing up graduate school and the other graduated a year ago. Their daddy purchased the exam popcorn locally and presented it personally. When he pulled the oversized tin from behind his back, they squealed and jumped up and down, delighted that the tradition continues.

Valentine's Day—No longer do they have shoebox construction paper covered mailboxes for this special day. This would be a good time to collect lots of red and white surprises and make a small care package. Conversation hearts will be a hit!

Whatever the occasion, if you are sending a care package, remember that most college students still practice what they learned in kindergarten. They may not hold hands any more when they cross the street; however, they are making new friends; they are nice to one another; and they *always* share. So send plenty!

College Birthdays

Birthdays away from home can seem less than adequately celebrated. But there are ways to contribute to the festivities even if your child is in college.

Of course, this is a good time for a package. Do your best to see that it arrives on the proper day. Remember though, some college post offices are not open on the weekends.

Organize an email campaign. Tell all his friends, your friends, and neighbors to help "shower" your child with email messages. Send them an email that includes the date of the birthday and the email address. Then it will only take a minute to send a greeting. Be sure to tell them to put Happy Birthday and the child's name in the subject line so it will not be deleted.

If the college or university is close enough, surprise your student with a favorite lunch. Ginger attended a college about an hour away from home. On her first birthday there, I showed up with Chinese food from her favorite Chinese restaurant. The owner was happy to come to his restaurant early and fix an assortment of the things he thought college students would like. Then he packed it for traveling. Ginger's face was total shock and extreme pleasure when she saw the table surrounded by friends set with Uncle Poon's! She has never forgotten that birthday party!

If you are not close enough to provide a "party," you can still help with the celebration. Talk to a friend and find out your child's favorite place to eat in the town where the college is located. Then get a gift certificate for your student and a friend or two to enjoy eating there on his birthday. Call during the time they will be eating so you can "sing" your greeting.

Find out if the college makes any provision for birthdays. Perhaps the kitchen staff can provide a cake. Or there may be an organization with an ongoing project to provide birthday celebrations for students on campus.

Don't be too hard on yourself if you can't be there. Your student knows that with the transition to college came the realization that some things, such as birthday celebrations, may have to be done differently. Through the years you have laid a good foundation for the relationship you have with your student. Your child knows that if you can't be there to celebrate the birthday in person, you are home wishing you were!

When Your Child Takes a Trip

Children love to have new experiences, and most children do very well when traveling away from mom and dad. But while they are gone, remind them how special they are. It is nice for them to know they are missed as well, but if your child tends to get homesick, don't play up the fact that you miss him a lot. Focus on knowing that he is having a good time on his trip and doing lots of new things. Encourage him to remember every little detail so he can tell you about the trip when he returns home.

Trips could be with the family of a friend, with a church group, or with grandparents. When your child is packing the suitcase, hide a few notes in between the stack of underwear! If there is a mailing address where he is going, send a card just to say hi. If your child will be able to go shopping, enclose a dollar so he can pick out a favorite snack or small toy. Having a little bit of money to spend makes him feel grown up and independent.

Suitcase Note

I am so glad you got to go visit Grandma and Grandpa.
Have lots of fun and give them a hug for me. I love you!

A Lunchbox Kid says

The most special note I received from my mother wasn't in my lunchbox . . . It was in my suitcase when I was traveling on Choir Tour one year. She gave me a card a day to read while I was away . . . and this particular day she gave me a card that pretty much said that no one could or would ever love me

156

like she does. I knew right then and there that if I turned out to be half the woman my mother was I was going to be an awesome woman.

—Kellyn, age 19

Summer Camp

Love notes to summer camp can be just as important as love notes in the lunchbox. Mail Call is a very important time, whether at summer camp or church camp. Often there is quite a bit of prestige attached to having your name called as the mail is handed out. So whenever your child is away and within reach of a US Post Office, make sure to mail something to arrive at the appropriate time.

Before your child leaves home

Before you close the lid to the suitcase or trunk, make sure you include a few love notes hidden in strategic places.

1. Hide one in the stack of underwear. That's one place you hope he will look, and as he changes, the stack will be pared down!

2. In the pajamas or nightgowns is another good place. Surely, come nighttime, love notes there will be found.

3. If your child takes a soap dish and a bar of soap, take an ice pick or sharp knife, dip in hot water, and write "hi" or draw a smiley face directly on the soap.

4. If stationery is packed, slip a small note inside the paper pad saying, "Can't wait to hear how much fun you are having!"

5. And, of course, inside a shoe or sock!

6. Stickers can also be used to say "hi" in various places inside a suitcase or camp trunk.

The most important thing is that your presence is there. Even though you and your child are separated for a short period of time, she can be assured of your love, support, and prayers.

While at camp

Mail something frequently. Some welcome items are:

Cards. These can be store bought, computer generated, hand-made, or leftover from some other occasion.

My children have enjoyed my attempts at computer generated cards.

When I was first learning how to use a computer, my son went to church camp. Of course, he expected to get mail; he had received mail at camps all of his life. I decided this particular time I would impress him with my computer skills. He had been very patient in trying to teach me how to use our new home computer.

I decided what I wanted to say on the card, opened a desk top publishing program, and selected the type of card that I wanted. (I think I selected some sort of double fold thing.) I composed my verse and typed it in and hit print. The very first try it came out just as I had positioned it, but the entire card was about one inch square. I was not sure if I could fold something that small four times!

So I tried again. After selecting the type of card, I looked around for a way to size my creation. Discovering a new button, I hit print again. This time the four sides of the card printed on four separate sheets of paper!

I was frustrated, I really wanted to do this computer thing and impress not only my son but also his friends. There weren't many computer savvy moms at that time, and I knew the whole group would look at my card and go, "Wow!"

Well, I decided the effort was even more impressive than the card itself. So the first day he was at camp, I put the one-inch-square card into an envelope and mailed it along with a short note that said, "I tried. But maybe I need a few more lessons when you get home!"

The second day, I included the four-page model. My next note read, "Oops! I think I went a little too far in the other direction!"

By the third day, with a little help from Dad, I was able to print out a fairly decent customized greeting card and mailed it along with a "Success at last!" note.

Every now and then someone reminds me of my first attempt at computer cards. Occasionally, I try again now with much greater success.

I also try to recycle or reuse cards that are leftover. My mother used to buy cards and store them in a drawer until the corresponding occasion came along. Sometimes she would buy many more than she really needed. Other times, she couldn't find the correct card when it was time to send it. So, my sister and I "inherited" several drawers full of greeting cards. Instead of throwing them away, I use them when there is a need to mail a note and just cross through what is printed on the card to make it fit.

For instance, if the card says "Happy Birthday, Niece" I might cross out "Birthday" and write in "camp day." Then I cross out "niece" and write in "daughter." It actually looks pretty tacky, but it is a way to use up the cards I have on hand. I always try to add a little of my own art to the cards done this way so the children won't think they are getting leftovers! They actually think it's pretty neat sometimes!

Care Packages. This type of mail is always welcome. Just be sure you know the rules of the camps your children are attending.

When I was a camper, the camp did not allow any food in the cabins. So care packages could not contain any food. My mother knew this and she was very careful to find surprises that were not edible. (We had to open the packages in front of counselors so there was no way to smuggle food back to the cabin.) Mama found little games and cute stationery (hoping I would write her) and other items she thought I would like.

On church missions trips, my children always welcomed some of their favorite snacks. Just be sure to send enough for all those who will be around when the package is opened.

One year my daughters were on choir tour with our church. I wanted to do something they would enjoy and appreciate. One of their favorite snacks was my home-made peanut butter cookies. I decided to make homemade cookies and mail them to the girls along the way. The only problem was that there were 110 youth on that trip. So as fast as I could bake peanut butter cookies, Dad packed them. We sent hundreds of cookies through the mail as a surprise to the girls, and they enjoyed passing them out on all the buses.

Newsletters. Here's your chance to let the creative juices flow. If you don't want to try your hand at designing your own, your computer probably has a desktop publishing program that already has a newsletter template. That way you can put your own information into the program and have a ready-made newsletter.

When my niece went to camp (same camp I had to gone to years earlier, by the way) I knew how much fun it was to return to your bunk for rest hour and find a letter. I decided her second year to create a personalized newsletter. (See sample camp newsletter in appendix.)

Not sure what local news would be of interest to a nine-year-old, I created some of my own. For the first issue, the headline read "Sparkle City Not the Same Without Celia." The feature article was about the fact that something was missing in our town. It was silly, but it told Celia that she was being missed. It was done in a light manner so as not to spark any homesickness. Since I had a scanner, I was able to include pictures of Celia and her cousins. If your child has pets, the family dog or cat would make good picture messages. I also included a knock-knock joke, a Scripture verse, and a short message that I was praying for her. When her dad, my brother, told me of events she had reported from camp, I tried to incorporate those items into the newsletter.

For instance, one camper fell in cheerleading class and hit her head. So I included an article in the next issue about how dangerous cheerleading was. And, of course, the fact that Celia was participating and I hoped the rest of the class would be injury free!

Celia and her cabin mates loved the newsletters. One day her dad called on the telephone.

"Have you heard from Celia?" I asked.

My brother laughed and said, "Yeah, we had a letter from her. All she talked about was your newsletter!"

Special Notes. Notes don't have to be long to say a lot! Mail a blank page of paper one day. Enclose a note (or even mail it in a different envelope) that says:

It's pretty empty at home without you. Just like this blank page! There is not much noise, either. The quietness reminds me of how much I love your laughter and noise. Yes, your noise!

Just the sound of you being nearby brings me joy!
I'm glad you are having so much fun and enjoying
beautiful Camp Watchey Mountain. See you soon!

Look for newspaper articles your camper would enjoy. Clip and put in an envelope and mail. No note is even necessary for that day! Just the fact that you took time to clip and send says you are thinking about your camper!

A Lunchbox Kid says

I had a note in my duffle bag at our church's camp. It said:

Dear Mikala,
The house it already quieter here now that you've left! Believe it or not your brothers are really missing you! I hope you learn a lot about God and all His wonders there. Try to stay away from the guys!!

Love,
Mom and Dad

—Mikala - age 12

Job Interview

Many students today have part-time jobs after school. These are treated no differently than other jobs. They must go through the application and interview process. When being interviewed for a job, your child must rely on his self-confidence to give him the poise he needs to speak with prospective employers. You have been contributing to this self-confidence from the day he was born. Every word of encouragement and every love note in his lunchbox has helped to build self-confidence and self-esteem.

Don't overdo your support for the day. Just the thought of having a job interview is enough to over-whelm a teenager. Ask pertinent questions once. Hopefully, just by answering a few questions, your child will tell you lots of information. A love note in the lunch-box or car will encourage your child and can be read over and over if your child becomes nervous.

When your children are older and ready to enter the workforce full time, some of the same principles apply.

Above all, make sure your child knows of your uncon-ditional love. No matter what the outcome of this job interview, your child is doing a great job of the number one job—that of being your son or daughter!

When Mama Goes Out of Town

It's rare at our house for me to leave town without Dad. But being absent for a few days is a prime note-writing opportunity. When I leave home, either for business or for pleasure, it is important for me to leave my "mark," for my presence to remain despite my absence.

Stickers

Just as you used stickers in the lunchbox to convey a quick message, stickers strategically placed will have the same effect. Since a rose sticker is my signature sticker I use lots of those! Think of the places your child (or husband) will look each day. Put a sticker on the bathroom mirror so he will see it when brushing his teeth. Stick one to the top pair of underwear or in the pajama drawer. If your child has a sports event while you are gone, a sticker on a piece of sports equipment will bring a smile. Small stickers will fit on the toothbrush or hairbrush handle. Don't forget the inside of the medicine cabinet. It's a welcome surprise to come to the end of the day, tired and ready to go to bed, and open the cabinet and find a "love note."

Candy Notes

Candy notes are also welcome while you are gone. On one occasion I bought a bag of chocolate kisses and made a card on the computer that said, "Here's a kiss from Mom." I made multiple copies, attached a "kiss" and placed them all over the place—in drawers, in shoes, on the pillow, everywhere I could think of. I used the entire bag that trip!

Snail Mail Notes

If time allows before I leave and I am going to be gone several days, I arrange to have notes arrive in the mail during my absence. This takes a little planning and usually requires mailing something the day before I leave, in which case there is not much "news." So I write a short note or compose a short poem about what a neat kid my child is. Usually I arrange for a friend to mail the notes because I am more secure in the arrival date if I know they are mailed in town. That also avoids the possibility of a meeting running too late to get it in the mail on the right day, etc. Bought cards can simplify this task, computer cards work, or a combination.

Annie

For a year, we had a child from India to live with us as a part of our family. Kim fit right in with our children, and that year was a highlight in our family life.

Another family living near us also had a child from India. Because the mother in that home was a teacher and had to leave very early to be at school, I picked up Annie, their India child, for school each day.

One day we were running late, and my children had a hard time getting all their school stuff together. We dashed out the door to school, without giving Annie a thought! When we arrived at school, Kim was greeted with "Where's Annie?"

Oops! I jumped back in the car and ran back to our neighborhood to pick up Annie.

The next morning as we got ready to leave the house, my whole family chanted, "Don't forget Annie! Don't forget Annie!" Even during breakfast, Annie was the topic of conversation.

Finally ready, we dashed out the door and, with one glance at my car, broke into gales of laughter. Tied to my car's antenna was a huge bouquet of yellow balloons. On the middle balloon was written one word—*Annie*.

I didn't forget her that day or any other because of that creative note. Though the "balloon note" was short, its message was loud and clear and delivered in a way that didn't make us feel bad about our mistake but made sure we didn't forget again!

Honeymoon

Years ago, when I left with my new husband on my honeymoon, the first time I reached into my purse for a piece of gum, I found an envelope with a small folded piece of paper in it. Recognizing my father's handwriting, I pulled it out and eagerly opened it. I thought perhaps he had slipped in a bit of "hot dog money" as a special surprise. But inside that envelope was something much more valuable. It was a note declaring his constant love for me and assuring me that our love would remain the same despite my new name. I have that note today and often reread it. And although it is decades old, it never ceases to bring a smile to my face and an occasional tear to my eye!

When I recently mentioned this to my children, my married daughter said, "I still have the love notes you both put in my suitcase when I left for my honeymoon, too!"

Even though your son or daughter may have moved on to establish a new household, your love and support is appreciated even more. When you write love notes to your married children, don't forget their spouses. Instead of now writing a joint love note or letter, take time to write the new spouse a separate note. He or she will appreciate being treated as one of the kids!

Lunchbox Challenge—A Final Word

I hope you feel challenged to try a few of these ideas. Even more than that, I hope you feel determined to work harder to encourage those around you.

Your lunchbox kid may be about ready to leave the nest. But just because your laundry loads are lighter, your responsibilities as a mom, wife, and encourager are not. No matter what stage of life your family is currently in, a word of encouragement is always timely and welcome.

In Isaiah 61:3, Isaiah tells us that we are *a planting of the Lord for the display of His splendor*. Some people easily and openly display His splendor in large groups. Others of us prefer the quiet, one-on-one moments with family members or friends.

A love note, whether in a lunchbox or on the windshield of a car, can display God's splendor in a very special way. Can you think of someone who might need a special touch today?

Appendix

Tips for Writing Notes

Notes do not have to be wordy. A few well-chosen words will do for most days.

Notes do not have to be profound. Just the fact that you took time to write says a lot.

It's OK to say the same thing on more than one day . . . just don't say it two days in a row!

It is not what you say; it is that you say something.

Remember that a great percentage of what you write will end up in the lunchroom trash, so don't spend an enormous amount of time crafting an artistic masterpiece.

A note written on anything will do; you don't have to have formal notepaper.

The entire family can get involved in writing lunchbox love notes. Mom can write one day and Dad the next. Even the family cat and dog can get into the act. Having a different writer occasionally will be fun for your lunch-box child.

Do not feel like you are competing with other moms and dads. Say what it is that *your* child needs to hear.

For younger children (kindergarten and first grade) every note may say "I love you." The trick may be to find creative ways of saying it! During the second half of the year, they will probably be better readers and you can add more words.

Words to Build Name Acrostics

A — awesome, amazing, astounding, attractive, adorable, athletic

B — brainy, beautiful, brave, bold, brilliant

C — cute, charming, compassionate, courageous, clever, caring

D — delightful, dear, dedicated, devoted, darling, daring

E — energetic, excellent, efficient, easygoing, enthusiastic, exciting

F — fun, funny, friendly, famous, fabulous

G — gracious, great, gregarious, genuine, good, gentle

H — helpful, healthy, honest, happy, hard-working

I — important, insightful, intelligent, interesting, irresistible

J — jolly, just, joyful, jovial, jubilant

K — kind, keen, kingly, kid

L — loving, laughing, lovely, lively, leader

M— maternal, moving, muscular, marvelous

N — nocturnal, nice, newsy, nifty

O — open, obliging, outstanding, original

P — pleasant, polite, pure, pleasing, patient
Q — quality, queen, quick
R — right, rare, respectful, royal, responsible
S — sociable, sweet, sunshine, smart, sympathetic
T — talkative, tireless, tidy, tender, thoughtful
U — unbelievable, upright, unique
V — victorious, valuable, virtuous
W — wise, warrior, witty, wonderful
X — Xcellent! Xciting!
Y — young, youthful
Z — zany, zestful. zealous

Note Prompts

• You are like your mama/daddy because . . .
• You make me proud when . . .
• Today is going to be a great day for you because . . .
• Every time I see you (*being kind to your brother, helping without being asked, smile and bat your baby blues, etc.*), I love you even more.
• I can't wait for you to get home because . . .
• You are my favorite son/daughter because . . . (only use this one if you have only one son or daughter!)
• You are my favorite soccer (football, basketball, tennis) player because . . .

Blank Love Notes

For you to photocopy and personalize.

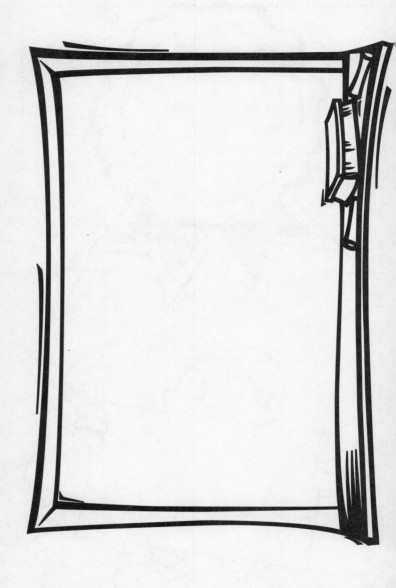